THE BEFORELIFE OF ELIZA VALENTINE

LAURA PEARSON

Boldwood

First published in Great Britain in 2024 by Boldwood Books Ltd.

Copyright © Laura Pearson, 2024

Cover Design by Lizzie Gardiner

Cover Imagery: Shutterstock and Adobe Stock

Every effort has been made to obtain the necessary permissions with reference to copyright material, both illustrative and quoted. We apologise for any omissions in this respect and will be pleased to make the appropriate acknowledgements in any future edition.

A CIP catalogue record for this book is available from the British Library.

Paperback ISBN 978-1-83603-445-2

Large Print ISBN 978-1-83603-446-9

Hardback ISBN 978-1-83603-444-5

Ebook ISBN 978-1-83603-447-6

Kindle ISBN 978-1-83603-448-3

Audio CD ISBN 978-1-83603-439-1

MP3 CD ISBN 978-1-83603-440-7

Digital audio download ISBN 978-1-83603-443-8

Boldwood Books Ltd
23 Bowerdean Street
London SW6 3TN
www.boldwoodbooks.com

For Lauren North, Nikki Smith and Zoe Lea.
You know why.

PROLOGUE
JULY 2021

When my parents met for the first time, I was watching. They met at a party, in a garden, and my siblings and I were hovering nearby, unseen. Samuel, more soulmate than brother. Thomas, the quietest and most contemplative of the four. Me, Eliza. And finally Lucy, my sharp and smart little sister.

But that meeting with Ryan, my father, wasn't the start of it. The start was a few months before, when our mother met Anthony.

I saw eighteen-year-old Anthony Winters turn a corner – walking backwards, the way teenage boys sometimes do – and bump into seventeen-year-old Becca Valentine with a muffled thud. Could it have been on purpose? I think so. I saw the notebook fall from Becca's hands and drop to the floor, loose photocopies of biological diagrams of the heart scattering. Anthony apologised, touched Becca's arm and checked – once, and again – that she was okay. He bent to pick up the notebook, gathered the papers, handed it all back to her with an easy smile. And when he walked away, Becca stood quite still and watched him until he was out of sight.

It was July, the last week of the school year. Everything was winding down. Outside, we'd heard, it was muggy.

'He's the one,' Lucy said excitedly. 'Our father.'

I was shocked. We'd been told that we would know our father when we saw him. I'd never considered that we wouldn't all have the same one. 'No,' I said. 'No, he isn't.'

I had nothing against this tall and quietly handsome boy, with a sureness to his step that belied his age. But he was not my father.

'He's mine,' Thomas said.

I turned to Samuel. My Samuel. My first and best friend. He shook his head.

And suddenly, where once there had been four people, united, there were now two pairs. Samuel and me. Lucy and Thomas.

We'd been there, hovering and watching, for seventeen years. Arriving when our mother, Becca, was born. Our bodies and faces human but indistinct, like an outline sketched in pencil. We could see our mothers and everyone else who'd already been born, but they couldn't see us. We're called Almosts. And this life we're living? It's called the Beforelife.

1

JULY 2021

By the time Becca met Anthony, we'd seen her learn to walk, watched over her first day at school, witnessed her first kiss. But this was the biggest moment yet. This man was Lucy and Thomas's father, but not mine. Not Samuel's. I was shaken.

I'd always felt closer to Samuel, right from the start. I'd thought it was because of how thoughtful he could be, how caring he was. But perhaps this was why. We were going to share a father. Or, at least, we weren't going to share the same father as the others. But where was the sense in it? Thomas and Lucy had the same father but my conception date was in between theirs. The one piece of information we'd always known, in addition to our names, was our conception dates. We'd worked out early on that Becca was going to be a young mother if she was going to be a mother at all. All of our dates fell within six years, between her seventeenth and twenty-third birthdays. But we'd always had hope. And with this revelation, it felt like everything had been thrown up in the air, and instead of landing, had scattered and blown about.

* * *

Later, Samuel came to check on me. Lucy and Thomas weren't around. It was often like this. Essentially, we Almosts had two choices. We could watch our mothers, never straying more than a few metres away from them, or we could be nowhere, seeing nothing. Sort of switched off. Mostly, we chose that option when Becca was sleeping and there was nothing to see. But for some reason, Lucy and Thomas had chosen it that afternoon. Perhaps they knew that Samuel and I needed time alone.

'I don't know how to feel about it,' I said. 'I never considered that there would be more than one father.'

'Me neither.'

I waited for him to say more. It was like that, with him. He didn't rush. He made sure he had his words right before he said them.

Eventually, he continued. 'I think it's okay, Eliza. I mean, we've always known that some of us might not be conceived. That's the harder thing to take, right?'

'I feel like our chances have just taken a knock,' I said.

'How so?'

'Well, because Thomas and Lucy have the same father but they're not going to be born in sequence. I'm in between them. For us all to make it, she'd have to go back and forth between two men and that just seems... unlikely.'

Samuel didn't say anything for a minute or two. And when he spoke, it was a single word. 'Yes.'

We were silent for a while. It was easy to be silent with him. For the hundredth time, I wished I could rest my head on his shoulder, the way we'd seen people do. It looked, to me, like the most comforting of ways to be with another person. But we weren't people yet, so we could only soothe one another with words.

'Are you scared?' I asked.

'About leaving here? Not scared, no.'

There were three months to go until Samuel's date. He'd always been impatient to get to it, while lately I'd been clinging to the hours, willing them to stretch.

'But what if...?' I couldn't finish the question. It hung there, between us, and I wished I could reach out and grab it. Un-ask it.

'I'm not scared of disappearing. I'm sad to be leaving you. But not scared. I won't know anything about it, will I?'

I shook my head. Nobody knew, for sure, but we assumed that if you missed your date, and disappeared, that was the end of everything, and there was no feeling nor knowing.

The rules of the Beforelife were passed down from Almost to Almost. Any woman's Almosts were visible to us if we really concentrated. When Becca was born, when we appeared, her parents had two more Almosts, Sarah and Charles, and they gave us a crash course on how it all worked.

'You have a conception date but it doesn't mean you'll be conceived,' Sarah said.

'What?' I didn't understand.

'You're an Almost. The four of you, you represent the times Becca's going to come closest to conceiving a child. She might have some of you, or all of you, but she might not.'

We were silent, taking it in. And then Samuel spoke.

'Will we remember all this, if we get to be born?'

Sarah looked at Charles, and he was the one to answer us.

'No.'

'How do you know?' Samuel asked.

'Because all of them' – he gestured with his arm and we understood that he meant everyone in the world – 'they've all been here, all been Almosts. And none of them ever mention it.'

Over time, we learned that what he said was true. And there were more questions, always more. For a while, we saw Sarah and Charles as an extension of our little group, only wiser. But their dates came and went, first hers, then his, and they disappeared. Becca remained an only child.

There was one more tool that we had at our disposal, and none of us had used it yet. Every Almost got one Chance to be a part of their mother's world, to inhabit someone's body for a while. We could use it however we wanted, but Almosts typically used it to increase their chances of being conceived. Smoothing over a rift between the potential parents. Talking someone with cold feet into going through with a wedding. That sort of thing.

'Have you thought about how you'll use your Chance?' I asked Samuel, then.

'Not really. It's too early, isn't it? I think I need to see how things stand in the final few days.'

'I wish she'd hurry up and meet your father,' I said. 'Before it's too late.'

'Me too, and I hope my father is your father,' he said.

I hoped that too.

* * *

The next day, on the walk to school, Becca seemed like she had a little too much energy. She kept going ahead, waiting for her best friend Ellie to catch up, starting conversations and then losing interest. The sky was clear, the summer holiday mere days away. The four of us trailed behind the girls, along with Ellie's Almosts, five boys who we'd known forever, all of whom were due to be born years after us.

'What's going on?' Ellie asked.

Becca smiled, dipped her head. 'Do you know Anthony Winters in the year above?'

Ellie looked thoughtful, like she was running a list in her head. Her older brother Josh seemed to have played football with everyone. 'Dark hair, kind of long. Looks a bit like he should be in a band. Hangs out with Luke Brady. That one?'

Becca nodded. 'I think I like him,' she said.

Ellie smiled. 'You might be a bit late with that. He's about to leave, isn't he?'

Becca stopped walking. It was clear she hadn't thought of that. 'I wonder whether he's going away to uni.'

Ellie shrugged, pulling on her friend's arm to get her moving again. 'I bet he is. He's clever. He won some English prize once, went up in assembly. Remember?'

Becca shook her head. They'd reached school by then and were about to part to go to their separate tutor rooms for registration.

'Him?' Ellie asked, with a slight incline of her head.

We all turned and saw him. Anthony. Striding across the quad, his hands in his pockets. I had a sudden memory of Becca's dad telling her not to walk like that when she was small, telling her she would need to put her hands out in front of her if she fell. I looked at her eyes, saw that she was falling now, in a different way.

'Why have I never noticed him before?' Becca asked. 'I mean, he's hot, isn't he?'

Ellie wrinkled her nose. 'If that's your thing,' she said.

Becca laughed. They didn't like the same boys, never had. It had been a blessing for their friendship.

* * *

When Becca got home from school that afternoon, her parents were arguing. We could hear them before she opened the back door, and she stood for a moment with her key in the lock, listening. But their angry voices were muffled, so she turned the key and went inside, and they were in the kitchen, their faces red and twisted. Both of them turned to her in unison as she came through the door. They went silent, lowered their heads.

'Don't stop on my account,' Becca said. She grabbed an apple from the fruit bowl and went upstairs to her room.

Becca probably didn't remember a time before the arguments, but we did. In the early days, Dave and Liz Valentine had been in love. Once, while Becca was napping in her Moses basket, they had danced in the living room and Dave had twirled his wife and then caught her in his arms and told her he was the luckiest man alive. But it hadn't lasted, and by the time Becca was going to school, things were strained. They'd begun to live separate lives. And then last year Covid had come along and thrown families into closer proximity than usual, and the arguments had stepped up.

Becca lay on her bed and I expected her to put her headphones on and listen to music or watch a film, but she didn't. She must have been trying to listen. Dave was saying something about 'one more year' and Liz was saying she wasn't sure she could do it. I didn't know what they were talking about. Did Becca? I watched a tear slide down her face, then another. And

I wished, as I always did, that I could reach out and touch her, tell her that it would be okay.

There was a knock on her door then, and her dad put his head into the room.

'How was your day?' he asked. 'I'm sorry you walked into that.'

'What's going on?' Becca asked.

Dave sat down on the chair beside Becca's desk and his face reddened a little.

'We're not getting on...' he said.

'You never get on. What's it about this time?'

'Nothing new,' he said. 'I'm just sorry you overheard it. It isn't fair.'

I thought Becca was going to snap back at him, saw that she had the words stored and ready to go, but she didn't. Perhaps because of how terribly sad he looked.

'What's going on with you?' he asked.

Would she tell him about Anthony? No, I didn't think so.

'Nothing much,' she said. 'Got History coursework to do.'

'Better make a start on it then.' And then he stood up and left the room, pulling the door closed quietly behind him.

When Becca's mum called her down for dinner, her dad was gone. Becca didn't ask where. I thought he was probably out in the shed, which he escaped to often. He made small pieces of furniture and toys from wood, and sold them at local craft fairs. It wasn't about the money, though. It was about the time, the space.

Liz had made macaroni cheese, and the two of them ate it in near silence, sitting opposite one another. Becca scrolled through Instagram and TikTok on her phone. For years, there'd been a family ban on phones at the table, but it hadn't been enforced for a while.

When Becca broke the silence, her voice sounded a little too loud. I could tell it had cost her something to speak, that she'd had to muster the courage. 'I heard Dad say something about one more year.'

She didn't ask a question, just let the statement hang there, inviting a response with her eyes.

Her mum put a hand to the back of her neck and rubbed, as if she had a pain she was trying to ease. 'It's nothing,' she said, her voice tight and clipped.

And Becca didn't ask again. We'd all learned that there was no point, sometimes.

I wondered whether it was times like this that she missed having a sibling. Her parents were a unit of sorts, even though they were so often at odds with one another, and they shut her out of the things they argued about. What difference would a brother or sister have made to her? All the difference in the world, it seemed to me. An ally, a friend. I thought of Sarah and Charles, how they might have filled that position, if they'd had the chance.

I looked at Samuel, saw that his expression was pained.

'They're going to split up,' Lucy said, and we all turned to her.

It was as if we thought she could possibly have some inside information that the rest of us weren't privy to.

Lucy shrugged. 'I'm telling you,' she said.

Becca's phone pinged and we all looked over her shoulder to read the message from Ellie:

> Anthony's going to Bristol after the summer.
> Sorry to be the bearer of bad news.

Becca looked at it for a long time. She didn't reply.

I waited for Samuel to speak. Knew, somehow, that he would.

'There's still time, isn't there, Eliza, for her to meet someone else?' he asked, his voice quiet. It wasn't the kind of thing we could talk about with Lucy and Thomas, now that we were rooting for different things. Now that there were sides, and lines, and different fathers.

'Plenty of time,' I said. But I didn't know whether I believed it.

2

SEPTEMBER 2021

Becca passed the summer with Ellie in parks and pubs, and it was such a contrast from the previous summer, when everyone had been in lockdown. I had high hopes for her meeting someone on one of the long, lazy days or sunlit evenings. But there was nothing. They talked about Anthony a few times, and each time, we were all on high alert, but they didn't see him, and nothing came of any of it. It was just the kind of talk they had while they were lying in one or other of their gardens on blankets, wasting time.

Before we knew it, school was starting up again, and it was their final year, and I assumed Anthony had been forgotten until Ellie brought him up out of nowhere on the walk to school one morning.

'Do you still like Anthony?' she asked. 'I saw him last night.'

Becca turned to look at her friend and her cheeks were a little flushed, and it was clear to all of us that there was still something there. But she didn't answer the question, just asked one of her own. 'Where?'

'I was out with my brother and we got talking to Luke, Anthony's friend. And then Anthony came over.'

'Why didn't you tell me?' Becca's voice was higher than usual, almost a squeal.

'Because it was only, like, ten minutes. And I'm telling you now. But anyway, he's not going to uni for another couple of weeks and my parents just happen to be going away for a couple of days at the weekend and I sort of...'

'What?'

'Well, I told him I was having a party. You should have seen Josh's face. But anyway, he's coming. You can thank me later.'

* * *

By the time the day of the party came around, word had spread pretty well. Becca went back to Ellie's house straight after school. There was work to be done. They put anything decorative or breakable in a big cardboard box and took it out to the garage. They moved all the yoghurts and cheese and vegetables in the fridge onto a single shelf to make room for drinks. They put the finishing touches to a party playlist and made sure the speakers in the kitchen and the living room were working.

'How can we make sure people stay downstairs?' Ellie asked.

Becca laughed. 'I don't think we can.'

Ellie looked panicked, and we saw Becca notice it. Saw her worry that Ellie might just call the whole thing off. Becca put her arms around her friend.

'People do this all the time. Remember the first party we went to?'

'Shauna Massey's,' Ellie said.

'Were we fifteen?'

'Must have been. You vomited red wine.'

'And you got with Dominic Reed.'

Ellie shuddered. 'Did we go upstairs?'

'Probably. Look, let's just let it all happen and then we'll sort it out afterwards. I promise. Have I ever let you down?'

Ellie rolled her eyes but didn't say anything. It was almost six. They both needed to get ready, and they hadn't eaten anything. Becca turned the oven on and pulled a pizza out of the freezer, while Ellie went upstairs to shower.

When the doorbell rang for the first time, they were sitting at the kitchen table with bottles of beer in front of them, untouched. Ellie jumped a little.

'Shall I get it?' Becca asked.

Ellie nodded. We followed Becca to the door, eager to see who it was, and when she pulled it open, Anthony was standing there, a cheap white carrier bag full of bottles of beer hanging from the fingers of one hand. Behind him, his friend Luke. Anthony smiled at Becca and she grinned back and didn't speak for a moment.

'Come in,' she said, finding her voice. 'You're the first.'

She showed them through to the kitchen and they put the beers they'd brought in the fridge and pulled out chairs from under the table.

'Who's coming?' Anthony asked.

Becca shrugged, despite the fact that she and Ellie had gone over who had been invited and who might turn up at least ten times.

'She doesn't care, now he's there,' Lucy said.

It was true, I thought, but callous of her to say it. I could feel Samuel's worry, growing like a living thing.

'We think about thirty,' Ellie said. 'Tasha and her lot from our year. Lucas and Matt and all of them.'

There was a beat of silence, and all four of them reached for their beers and put them to their mouths.

'Music!' Ellie said, remembering. She started the playlist and a Rihanna song burst into the room, too loud for the size of the group. Anthony and Becca shared a look and I wasn't sure what it meant, and then the doorbell went again, and pretty soon, the house was full.

Becca and Ellie were separated quite early on, both opening the door and showing people where the fridge was, but Anthony stayed close to Becca, and after an hour or so, when the house was full and everyone seemed to be having a good time, he slipped his hand into hers and pulled her towards the stairs and up them.

'What are you doing?' she asked, her voice light. She'd had a few drinks and she wasn't quite drunk but I could tell that she was looser, her inhibitions lowered.

'I want to talk to you,' he said. 'Where can we go?'

Becca nodded in the direction of Ellie's bedroom and Anthony opened the door and pulled Becca inside. They stood by the door after closing it for a minute or two, and I could see their chests rising and falling with their breaths. Their faces were inches apart but neither of them moved closer. And then, he reached out and touched her forehead very gently, brushing a lock of hair out of the way.

'Hello, Becca Valentine,' he said.

Becca smiled and lowered her head, and the hair he'd tucked neatly behind her ear came loose.

'Hello,' she said, almost a whisper.

'They're going to kiss!' Lucy said.

It lightened the moment, which felt monumental. Becca had kissed boys before, but this seemed entirely different. It seemed like the start of something big. And then they didn't kiss, because Becca moved away, ducking under his arm, and sat down on Ellie's desk chair. Anthony turned, leaning back against the door, his face all amusement. He crossed the floor and sat on Ellie's pristine bed. He beckoned her.

'It's okay,' I said, turning to Samuel. 'It might still be okay.'

He didn't answer. I'm not sure he could. I think we all expected Anthony to kiss Becca when she sat down beside him, but he didn't, not at first. He lifted the hand that she had resting on her thigh and interlaced his fingers with hers. I wondered how it felt, that touch. I wondered about warmth, and electricity, and all the things we'd heard about that we didn't – couldn't – understand.

'The first time I saw you—' he said.

Becca nodded. 'You mean when you didn't see me? When you walked into me?'

'No.' He smiled. 'Long before that. Last year. In the common room. You were sitting with Ellie and you had this necklace on and you were fiddling with it, pulling it back and forth on the chain.'

Becca pulled her hand away from his, lifted the silver chain she always wore from underneath her dress with finger and thumb.

'I asked Luke who you were,' Anthony said. 'He didn't know. And I've just... watched you.' He stopped, put a hand to his mouth. 'God, that sounds so creepy. I don't mean in a creepy way, I promise.'

Becca laughed and dropped her necklace, and I could see that she was waiting for Anthony to take her hand in his again. But he didn't.

'I had no idea,' she said.

'You must be the only one. It's like the worst kept secret in the school. And now, here you are...'

'Here we are,' Becca said.

And then we all knew, Becca and Anthony, and also Samuel and Lucy and Thomas, we all must have known, because it would have been impossible not to, that they were going to kiss. Anthony took his time, putting a finger under her chin as if to draw her to him. Every second felt stretched taut. Becca leaned in, slowly, slowly, and their lips touched and then it was like they were one person. His hands in her hair, their mouths moving slowly but with a great sureness, and when they pulled apart, they were both flushed, both breathing heavily. He smiled at her and she seemed so at peace, so unguarded and beautiful and fulfilled, that even I couldn't deny it.

'What am I going to do, Eliza?' Samuel asked me quietly, pleading.

'I don't know,' I said. 'I don't know.'

Was this it? The great love they all talked about; was it happening right in front of us? For the two of us, it was a potential disaster.

'Do you think we should go back down?' Becca asked.

But she didn't move; she stayed in his embrace while she was asking, and it was clear that she didn't want to go anywhere, that she'd just felt she should ask it.

'No, I don't,' Anthony said.

'Ten more minutes, and then I'll find Ellie, check things are okay,' Becca said, and she sounded like she was trying to convince herself.

They kissed again, slowly. They fell back together onto the bed and when they stopped kissing, they just lay side by side, on their backs, their hair mingled. They held hands. We all listened to the muffled thud of the music coming from downstairs.

'I hate this song,' Becca said.

'Me too. What *do* you like?'

Becca propped herself up on her elbow, facing him, and I could see she was trying to decide whether to be honest. Friends had laughed at her before when she had been. 'The Beatles,' she said.

Anthony looked surprised. 'No way! I love the Beatles!'

Becca smiled. 'Did you know that none of them could read music?'

'Everyone knows that.'

'I've never met anyone who does.'

They were grinning at one another, delighted. Anthony tipped over onto his side and pulled Becca towards him. Just then, the door burst open.

'Oh my god, there you are!' Ellie sounded sort of angry but mostly grateful. 'I've been looking for you everywhere. I need your help.'

'Mine?' Becca asked, sitting up.

'Both of you! I need you to help me get everyone out. It's massively out of control. There are people smoking in my parents' bedroom!'

Anthony stood and took hold of Becca's hand and they followed Ellie down the stairs like that, as if not being in physical contact would be too hard. The house was packed, more so than when Anthony and Becca had snuck off. In the kitchen, Anthony pulled out a chair from the table and stood on it, cupping his hands around his mouth.

'Guys, we have to get out of here. The police are on their way.'

There was something about his voice and his manner, quietly confident, that I admired. And I could see from Becca's face that she was in awe. Straightaway, people started moving towards the door. The music went off and there was a loud hum of voices, but they were on their way out. People came down the stairs, their clothes slightly crumpled and their eyes on the floor. And very soon, it was just Ellie and Becca, Anthony and Luke.

'Do you want us to go too?' Anthony asked. 'We could help clear up.'

Ellie sighed, the relief clear on her face. 'No, you can stay. And yes, please.'

The four of them went from room to room, opening the windows wide to air the place and picking up discarded bottles. Thanks to Ellie and Becca's sweep before the party started, nothing was broken. As they worked, Becca and Anthony kept looking over at one another covertly. And when it was done, he asked her to go for a walk with him. It was almost ten o'clock, the middle of September. Becca pulled a cardigan over her dress and stepped into her shoes.

'Are you leaving?' Ellie asked as Becca pulled open the front door.

'Just going for a walk. I'll be back in a bit.'

We followed them out.

'Is something going on between Ellie and Luke?' Thomas asked.

But no one answered. We were all too invested in what was clearly going on between Anthony and our mother. They held hands and walked down the deserted street, and near the cross-roads that would take them into or out of the town centre, Anthony pulled her into his body and kissed her lips very softly. They stood for a minute, her in his arms, her face buried in his jumper. I didn't need to see her face to know that she was happy.

'Which way?' he asked.

'The river?' Becca suggested.

The river ran behind the high street, and they walked in that direction, their hands joined. Becca led Anthony towards a little bench that was almost hidden by the hedgerow, and they sat at either end, studying one another.

'What's your favourite Beatles album?' he asked.

'*Sgt. Pepper's*. Yours?'

'*Revolver*. Why *Sgt. Pepper's*?'

'Because of "She's Leaving Home". Why *Revolver*?'

'Because of "Eleanor Rigby".'

'Did you know that Father Mackenzie was originally going to be Father McCartney?'

Anthony laughed. 'No, I didn't know that.'

Becca nodded and looked down to hide her face, and I could see that she was doing the kind of grin she did when she couldn't stop herself. When everything was just as right as it could be. She'd smiled like that on her sixth birthday when her dad had wheeled in a shiny, purple bike, and when she was going up to secondary school and found out that she and Ellie were going to be in the same tutor group.

Anthony reached down and picked a blue wildflower, leaned forward and tucked it into Becca's hair, behind her ear.

'I think you're perfect,' he said.

Becca let out a laugh that I knew meant she was nervous, or felt overwhelmed.

'There's no such thing,' she said.

'What are you sad about?' he asked.

Becca looked at him for a long time before answering. Was she sad? I didn't think so. But perhaps he could see and sense something in her, being with her like that, that I couldn't. It made me a little anxious.

'Sometimes I worry that nobody really knows me properly. I don't have any brothers or sisters, and my parents are always arguing or at work. I'm close with my dad, but I always censor what I say around him, the way you do with parents, you know? And then there's Ellie. We've been best friends since we were six, but there's stuff I'd never tell her...'

'Like what?'

'Like this feeling I have sometimes that I'm going to waste all my opportunities and have a shitty life. I don't know where it came from, but I think about it sometimes when I'm in the shower or just lying on my bed at night, and it scares me. I want to see everything, you know? Travel and learn about all different kinds of people. Or maybe not even that. I don't know. I just want to be happy.'

'I think you'll be happy, Becca Valentine,' he said, his voice low.

The river was moving so slowly that you had to watch it for a minute or two to really believe it was moving at all, and they sat there, not touching, their eyes straight ahead.

'Will you go out with me, next Friday night?' Anthony asked. 'I want to take you on a proper date.'

Becca looked in his direction. 'Yes,' she said. And then she leaned across and kissed his cheek before standing up.

'Next Friday is my date!' Samuel cried out. His voice was shrill and made me jump a little. I'd been so absorbed in the scene unfolding in front of us.

'Shit,' I said. 'What the hell are we going to do?'

He just looked at me, completely hopeless. I glanced over at Lucy and Thomas. They were happy with the way things were going, I could tell, but they were good enough to keep quiet about it.

'I have to go back,' Becca said. 'I'm staying at Ellie's. Which way do you live?'

'I'll walk you,' he said.

And all the way back, they were silent, sneaking kisses here and there. At Ellie's front door, Becca reached out and touched the stubble on his face.

'I feel like I'm going to miss you,' she said, and then she laughed a little, and I knew she was laughing in case what she'd said was too much.

'I know I'm going to miss you,' Anthony said.

He handed her his phone and asked her to put her number in it, and then he called her so that she had his.

'Goodnight,' he said, putting his arms around her waist and holding her close.

'Goodnight.' She pulled away, knocked on the door, and when she turned back he was just looking at her. 'Go,' she laughed. 'It's late.'

She slipped inside when Ellie came to the door, and they smiled at one another to acknowledge what had happened, and Ellie told Becca that Luke had just left, and that he'd kissed her, and they went into the kitchen to fill glasses with water. After Becca had brushed her teeth and changed into her pyjamas, she checked her phone one last time, and there was a new message, from Anthony.

Until next Friday, Becca Valentine.

And I wondered whether her face would start to ache from all the smiling.

* * *

I watched over her all that night, my mind turning things over. It was all going wrong. Becca hurtling towards a relationship with Lucy and Thomas's father, when they weren't due to be conceived for ages. And every day that passed, our time with Samuel was getting shorter. Whether he was conceived or not, we were about to lose him.

Deep in the night, Samuel came to me.

'Eliza, can I tell you something?' His voice was full of excitement, such a contrast to all the worry earlier, and I couldn't help but get swept up in it.

'Of course.'

'I've been trying something, with Becca. For months now. It's not much, but it's something. Come on, I'll show you.'

We looked around for Lucy and Thomas. They weren't there. At night, we usually stopped watching. Or at least most of us did. It seemed that Samuel had been using this dead time to work on this mystery project. I was terrified, and excited, and impressed.

Becca was asleep on a camp bed in Ellie's bedroom, her right arm flung off the side. I watched as Samuel got really close to her, closer than I'd ever been. He almost wrapped his body around hers. Why had I never done this, even when Becca had seemed like she needed comfort? The true answer was that I was afraid she'd feel my presence. But that was ridiculous. I waited and watched.

'Keep looking at her arm,' Samuel said.

I did. I flicked my eyes back and forth between her arm and his eyes, which were staring intently at her arm. And then, just when I'd stopped expecting anything to happen, it moved. She lifted it up and laid it across her stomach. Samuel was by my side in a moment.

'I did that!' he said. 'I've been dying to show you.'

I couldn't believe it. 'How? What do you do? Can you teach me?'

* * *

And that's how the tuition began. Each night, as soon as we'd shaken off our siblings, Samuel and I would spend long hours staring, focusing, trying to make things happen. It wasn't really something he could put into words, and that frustrated me. The first few tries, nothing happened. But I tried to relax about it. Tried to believe that it would come. And even if it didn't, I treasured that time with him as his days ran short. I'd never have thought of asking if we could spend the nights together, when Becca was asleep, but I loved that we did. When he was concentrating, showing me how he could make her move, I watched, trying to drink him in. I wanted to learn what he was teaching me, of course, but I just wanted to look at him, too. I wanted to cling to the best brother I might never have.

3

SEPTEMBER 2021

The next week passed in a flurry of messages between Becca and Anthony, and hushed conversations between Becca and Ellie that all revolved around Anthony and, to a lesser extent, Luke. Ellie liked Luke but there seemed to be a consensus between the girls that what was happening with Becca and Anthony was more significant. All of their focus was on that. Becca had told Ellie about their night together in great detail, more than once, and Ellie had gasped at the part about Anthony tucking a flower into her hair.

'It's like a bloody film!' she'd said.

And Becca had smiled and nodded. 'I know!'

'So do you think you'll get together properly? Even though he's going away?'

Becca shrugged. 'I have a good feeling. You don't have a night like that and then nothing.'

Ellie didn't say anything. The truth was, neither of them had had a night quite like that before.

* * *

It seemed to us like Friday came around fast, but Becca kept moaning to Ellie that the days were crawling by. Every time she checked her phone, there was another message from Anthony, and they all made her smile, or blush. Some of them she showed to Ellie and some of them she didn't. On Friday afternoon, they walked home together, as usual.

'What are you doing tonight?' Becca asked Ellie.

'I need to do my English coursework. Everyone's going to Kelly Dunne's party but I need to get some work done. What's the plan with Anthony?'

'We're meeting on the bench outside Boots at eight,' Becca said. 'That's all I know.'

'Do you think he has something really romantic planned?'

'I mean, if we were just going out for drinks, I don't know why he wouldn't just ask me to meet him in a pub. But I don't know. What do you think I should wear?'

They'd had variations of this conversation several times. I tuned out while they debated the possibility of being too dressed up or too dressed down. I was pretty sure Becca would end up in her favourite jeans and one of two or three tops that she wore on rotation for nights out.

I turned to Samuel and struck up a conversation we'd been having all week too. He looked defeated, like he'd already lost.

'You could stop it,' I said.

'What do you mean?'

'You could use your Chance, inhabit Anthony. Just make him... not turn up.'

Samuel sighed. 'I could. It just seems so cruel. Look how happy she is.'

'I know,' I said, 'but she doesn't know, does she? If she knew that going out with Anthony tonight would mean that one of her future children wouldn't get to be born, she might see it differently.'

He laughed, and I couldn't believe that he could, but then I stepped back and looked at it again and saw that it was quite funny, after all.

'But even if she doesn't go out with Anthony,' he went on, 'what are the chances of her meeting someone else and having sex for the first time, all before midnight tonight?'

I'd thought about this a lot, and it seemed like the chances were tiny. But I couldn't say that to him. 'I don't know,' I said instead. 'We *can't* know.'

We were quiet, looking at each other.

'I can't believe I might never get to touch you,' he said. 'It just doesn't make sense.'

'Will you try?' I asked, my voice giving away the weight of emotion behind the words. 'For me? Will you just try?'

'Okay,' he said. And he did this thing he did sometimes, where he laid his hand over mine. We couldn't feel one another, but I could imagine.

* * *

When Becca let herself in after school, her parents were sitting at the kitchen table in silence.

'What's going on?' she asked, reaching for a glass and opening the fridge to retrieve the orange juice.

'We want to talk to you,' her dad said. His voice was strangled, as if he didn't have full use of his throat.

'What about?'

'Just sit down,' her mum said. Her voice wasn't quite right either. And I tried to remember the last time I'd seen them sitting like this, just being. There had been a lot of it in the early years, but it felt like they'd spent the last decade circling one another to avoid a fight, or giving in and fighting. They had their safe spaces. For Dave, his shed, where he could easily pass half a day. And for Liz, the kitchen. That was where she wrote her shopping lists, prepared meals and, sometimes, sat at the table staring into space. Was she seeing a time when she'd been happy, I often wondered, or a different life altogether?

I could see that Becca had noticed things weren't quite normal. She put her glass of orange juice down on the table and pulled out a chair. And then she looked from one of them to the other, waiting.

'Your mum and me...' Dave began, but then he paused and looked over at his wife, as if pleading with her to do it. But she just looked down at the table, wouldn't meet his eye.

'They're splitting up,' Lucy said, and we all turned to her.

'Do you think?' Thomas asked.

'Yes. It's obvious.'

I didn't say anything, but what I wanted to say was that it was Samuel's date and that's what we should have been focused on. Not this, whatever this was.

'Are you splitting up?' Becca asked.

'We are, yes,' her dad confirmed.

Becca's eyes widened and I could see that, even though she'd said it, all bravado, she hadn't expected the answer to be yes. It was true that they fought, that they'd failed to get on for years, but that was just it. This situation wasn't new, and they'd never talked about ending their marriage before. Or at least, not to our knowledge.

'It was the lockdowns,' Lucy said, and I turned to look at her. 'Cooped up like that, and not allowed to see anyone else. That was the final nail.'

I didn't say anything. Becca looked like she was going to cry.

'I'm so sorry, love,' her dad said. 'But you must be able to see that it's not working, the way we're living. Things have been bad between us for a long time, but we always wanted to keep the family together...'

'And now?' Becca asked. 'Now you just don't want to any more?'

'No, we still want to. We just don't think we *can* any longer.'

He looked defeated. I turned to her mum, whose eyes were rooted to the table. She'd always been the lesser parent, less hands-on, less loving. It was just the way it was.

'Mum?' Becca asked. It was a plea.

'Your dad's right,' she said, finally looking up and making eye contact with her daughter. 'We can't go on like this. No one's happy.'

'I am,' Becca said. And then, almost a whisper, 'I was.'

Dave scraped back his chair and went to the cupboard for a glass, then to the sink to fill it with water. He didn't ask if anyone else wanted anything, and the fact that I noticed it made me realise that he always did. He was always checking whether everyone was okay, whether they needed him.

'I hope she gets to stay with him,' Samuel said.

It hadn't occurred to me, but it was obvious. If they were splitting up, one of them would be leaving. I, too, hoped that Dave would be the one to stay, because he and Becca were a team that worked and I couldn't imagine either of them functioning well without the other. But at the same time, something nagged at me. Becca had always fought for her mum's approval, for her mum to notice her more. What would she do if her mum left her? I wasn't sure I wanted to find out.

'So what's going to happen?' Becca asked, and her parents exchanged looks that were full of pleading and loss. It struck me that, after living with someone for almost two decades, you could have a conversation with them without words. But it wasn't enough, that ability. It wasn't the kind of thing that kept you together.

'I'm going to move out,' Becca's mum said. 'This weekend. I've found a flat in town.'

'This weekend?' Becca burst out. She stood up, went to the door. 'And you're only telling me now?'

'We didn't want to say anything until it was all sorted,' her dad said, sounding defeated. 'We know how hard this is going to be for you, and we just want to make it all as smooth as possible.'

Becca shook her head, as if trying to dislodge the information. There were tears on her cheeks. I wanted to reach out to her, offer her some comfort. She was sitting in a room with the two people who should love her more than anyone in the world, and she was in so much pain. It was awful to watch.

'You're so selfish!' Becca said, turning to her mum. 'This is what you've always wanted, isn't it? You've always been so horrible to Dad. I'm surprised he's put up with you this long, and now you'll be on your own, just how you like it. I don't know why you even had a child!'

I expected her mum to look broken, but her expression was fierce. 'Sometimes I don't know why either,' she said, her voice quiet but steady.

And that was the last we heard, because Becca shot up, left the room and raced up the stairs. But just before we followed her, I saw the look Dave gave his wife. The message he sent her. That what she'd said was unforgiveable. That it was a line that couldn't be uncrossed.

* * *

It was shortly after that that Samuel slipped away. I didn't notice at first. I was watching Becca, crying on her bed like her heart was in a thousand sharp and spiky pieces and wondering whether she'd go to meet Anthony after all. But after an hour of that, she'd cried herself out. She had a long shower, and when she came out, her eyes weren't quite so puffy. She opened her wardrobe door to reveal her full-length mirror, and then she sat on the floor with her makeup bag. I could always tell how important something was to her by how long she spent getting ready. That day, she took forever, wiping it all off and starting again not once, but twice. I kept trying to seek out Samuel, to exchange a worried look with him, and then realising he wasn't there. And it was a reminder, that this is how it would be. He wouldn't be here.

When her face was finally ready, she straightened and then slightly curled her hair and pulled out the clothes I'd predicted. She stood in front of the mirror, inspecting herself from different angles. It meant something, I thought, that despite what had just happened downstairs and how upset she was, she still cared about looking her very best for this date. I wanted Samuel to succeed in sabotaging it – of course I did – and yet a tiny part of me didn't. I wasn't sure how she'd take the heartbreak of Anthony not turning up on top of her parents' split. I wasn't sure how she'd get over it.

By six o'clock, two hours prior to their agreed meeting time, she was ready. She went down the stairs slowly, and I knew she was hoping to leave the house unnoticed. To avoid another confrontation that might make her cry again and undo all the work she'd done to make herself look her best. She was in luck. Her dad was in the lounge – we heard the TV as she snuck past the door – and her mum was nowhere to be seen. Becca pulled the front door shut behind her and hurried away from her house in the direction of town.

The next couple of hours felt long to us. Becca ate a burger and fries at McDonalds, she had a look in the window of several shops, she sat on a bench and sent messages to Ellie. She hadn't taken a jacket and she looked cold. She looked young and sad and alone.

'Why isn't she telling Ellie about her parents?' Thomas asked. 'She tells her everything.'

'She'll tell her tomorrow,' I said. I was sure of this. 'She needs to get through this date without getting upset again. She can't think about it.'

I wondered about Samuel. Where he was and what he was doing. When eight o'clock came around, Becca was standing behind the bench they'd agreed on, looking from left to right. I looked at her closely. You wouldn't know she'd been crying. Not from her eyes.

Even though I hoped Samuel was trying to make sure this date didn't happen, because his only chance of ever being born was Becca meeting his dad that evening, part of me was as anxious as Becca for Anthony to turn up. I felt that if he didn't, it might set something in motion, something ungovernable. And most of all, I just wished Samuel would come back. We had so little time left with him, and I missed him already.

At five past eight, Becca came around to the front of the bench and sat down. She checked her phone. At quarter past, she sent Ellie a frantic message.

He's not here!

Ellie replied in seconds.

> What? Have you messaged him?

Becca didn't reply straight away. She typed out a couple of different messages to Anthony and deleted them both. She went to call him and her finger hovered over the button for a few seconds, and then she cancelled it. Then she replied to Ellie.

> I can't do it. I can't bear to hear him come up with some excuse.

She watched her phone then, either for a message from Anthony or a reply from Ellie, but neither came. At half past, she looked like she knew. She stood up, stepped away from the bench, as if it would be shameful now to be found there, so long after the arranged time. I saw the tears gathering in her eyes and felt terrible for her, felt her pain as if it were my own. She sent Ellie another message.

> He's not coming. Fuck. do you want to do something?

Again, the reply was quick.

> Sorry, I've got so much coursework to do. But come over tomorrow or something, yeah?

Becca wrapped her arms around herself, as if for protection, and started to walk away from the bench.

'Do you think she'll go home?' I asked.

'No,' Lucy said. 'I don't think she will.'

And she didn't. She just walked, and at first I thought it was aimless, more a need not to go home than a need to be anywhere, but it became clear that she knew exactly where she was heading. Where she usually turned left to go home, she went right. And soon she was in the heart of a housing estate and turning a corner to reach a house that was pulsing with music and bodies. I watched the door open and people spill out, as if the house simply couldn't contain them.

'She's never been here before, has she?' Thomas asked.

'I don't think so,' I said. 'It must be that party Ellie mentioned. Kelly someone.'

'Dunne,' Lucy said quietly. 'Kelly Dunne.'

Becca headed inside without a backwards glance and into the kitchen where she opened the fridge and took out a bottle of wine. Someone passed her a plastic cup and she filled it and then drank, looking around her, presumably for a familiar face.

It was then that Samuel returned. 'Is she okay?' he asked.

'No,' Lucy said, her voice cold. 'She's gone to a party where she doesn't know anyone, and she's drinking.'

I turned to him, both of us thinking the same thing. There was still a chance for him.

'Listen, Eliza,' Samuel said, 'I might not have long. But that thing we've been trying to do, with Becca. Keep practising. Do it with me if I'm born. Use me to make sure you're born, too.'

'What do you mean?' I hadn't thought much beyond the fun of it, having someone you could move around at will, as if you were playing with a giant doll's house.

'I mean, it's like having extra Chances. You can make people go where you want them to, make things happen. It might help. I'll do everything I can to remember you. Everything.'

I was panicked. We should have talked about it before, and for longer. We'd had all those years, and now we were down to our last few hours, and it didn't seem possible.

'What was it like? Being there?' I asked in a rush. I didn't have long left to ask him everything that came into my head, the way I always had.

Samuel gazed at me, as if deciding how much to reveal. 'It's wonderful,' he said. 'It's like magic. I hope you get to experience it, Eliza. There are all these smells and textures, and everything's brighter than it seems from here, and louder.'

'And what did you do, as Anthony?'

'I crashed his mum's car.'

'What?'

'Just a scrape. No one got hurt. But he had to go back and face his parents, who were fuming because it was brand-new, and they made it clear he wasn't going anywhere this evening. And then I stopped him from messaging her.'

'What if he messages her now you're back?' I asked.

Samuel shrugged. 'I don't know. I didn't choose to come back. I guess I'd used up my time. So what he does now is out of my hands.'

We were silent then, and it felt like a waste of the little time we had left, but I didn't know what to say. Didn't know how to break it. I kept my eyes on him, as if I thought he might disappear at any moment, and then I remembered that it was Becca I needed to watch. It was her who held all the power, although she didn't know it. So I turned my attention back to the kitchen, where she was reaching for another drink.

4

SEPTEMBER 2021

Becca took her second cup of wine out into the garden. And then she stood with her back to the wall of the house, her eyes closed. We saw him before she did. There weren't many people outside. Two little clusters, and him. Standing alone. I turned to Samuel.

'It's him!'

He just nodded.

Lucy and Thomas spoke together. 'Your dad?'

'Our dad,' I said.

I was so relieved to finally learn that we shared him, Samuel and me. Even though we didn't know what would happen, or whether either or both of us would make it into their world, it was enough, just then, to know that we had the same mum and dad, that we were true brother and sister. That the bond I'd always felt with him was born of something physical and real. Was, perhaps, inevitable.

We didn't know his name, not until he said it. He walked across the small garden to where Becca was standing and waited for her to look at him.

'I'm Ryan,' he said.

'Becca.' She took another slug of wine and said nothing else, but I saw her noticing him, this boy – no, this man, who had come over to talk to her.

I was noticing him too. I couldn't take my eyes off him. He looked a few years older than her, and he had short, neat hair that was almost black and a look in his eyes that said he knew how attractive he was, knew how people wanted him. He was all stubble and straight teeth and wide jaw. Magnetic.

'Are you okay, Becca?' he asked.

And that was all it took for her to break. A tear fell, and then another, and Ryan moved closer and gathered her up in his arms and held her for a long time without saying anything.

When he did speak, his voice was thick. 'Let's go somewhere and talk,' he said.

She followed him inside the house and up the stairs, and he pushed open doors until he found a deserted bedroom.

'I don't know who you are,' Becca said, her voice a little croaky. 'I haven't seen you before. Did you go to our school?'

She sat down on the bed, and Ryan sat on a chair in the corner of the room.

'My brother is at school with... Kelly, is it? He said I should come along.' He shrugged. 'I thought there might be some more people my age here. I was about to leave, but then...'

'But then?' Becca looked up at him, her face still tear-streaked but her voice back to normal.

'Then I saw you.'

Becca blushed a little, but he kept looking at her and she didn't look away. And then he moved over to the bed, where she was sitting, and he sat down beside her and kissed her.

'Do you think...?' Samuel asked.

He didn't finish; couldn't, probably. But I knew what he was asking me. Did I think there was a chance for him, still? Did I think it was likely that in the next – I checked the clock on the wall – two and a half hours, Becca and this man, this stranger, would have sex? That she would do this thing she'd never done with anyone before, because she was sad about her parents splitting up and the boy she really liked not turning up for their date after the most romantic evening she'd ever had? Yes, I did.

I nodded. I wished I could reach out and hold him. 'Yes,' I said. 'Yes, I think so.'

After the kiss, they lay side by side. Just a week ago, she'd lain like this with Anthony at Ellie's house. It seemed like more than seven days had passed. She seemed older, more world-weary. And she was, I suppose.

'Tell me why you're sad,' Ryan prompted.

And she did. She told him that her parents were splitting up, that they'd always argued but she'd never thought it would come to this, somehow. She told him what her mum had said, that she didn't know why she'd had her. Ryan breathed in sharply when she told him that bit. But he didn't say anything. He let her speak. When her phone beeped with a message, she went to pull it from her pocket, but Ryan stopped her. I could feel Samuel's gaze on me, but I couldn't look away.

'Let's pretend it's just us, for tonight,' he said. 'Let's ignore everyone else.'

And Becca smiled and slid the phone back and didn't touch it again.

'I'm sorry,' Ryan said, 'about your parents. About your mum. It sounds horrible.'

'It's just, we've never been close, me and my mum. My dad's the one I'm close to, and he's never let me down. Ever. But for some reason, it's her I want approval from. It's stupid, but all my life I've been waiting for her to turn into the mum I need her to be. Thinking that she'll properly see me and realise she needs to step up and take care of me. I've been waiting since I was a little girl and part of me still is. And now this, basically admitting she wishes she'd never had me, and leaving.'

I thought she would cry again but she didn't. She looked more angry than sad.

'Forget about them, about her. Just for tonight.'

Becca managed a smile. She must have wondered what was happening, I thought. She hadn't had a love life of any kind, really, a week ago, and now all this. There had been Anthony admitting he'd been waiting for an opportunity to talk to her for a long time, and then letting her down spectacularly when she really needed him. And out of nowhere, this handsome stranger heaping attention on her.

'I don't trust him,' Lucy said.

I snapped my head round to look at her. Already, I felt fiercely protective of him, of this blossoming relationship, or whatever it might be.

'He's looking after her,' I said.

'Eliza, he's going to have sex with her and then disappear,' she said.

I thought about that. If it was true, then why would I exist? If this night was the only one Becca would spend with this man, the night they would conceive Samuel, then why would she have the potential to have another child with him later on? It didn't make sense.

I didn't answer Lucy. There was nothing to say.

'I think you're beautiful,' Ryan said. 'You have no idea, do you? You're just walking around, not knowing how beautiful you are.'

'You sound like a One Direction song,' Becca said, and she laughed.

He kissed her again. It was a different kind of kiss, this time. A searching one.

I didn't like watching people kissing, never had. It just looked so strange. So much like an invasion. And yet I knew, from the way Becca responded, that she liked it. I felt suddenly impatient, desperate to know how these things felt when you were inside a body and they were happening to you.

Becca pressed her body against his and kissed him back, and after a while, he reached beneath her top and undid the clasp on her bra and she didn't move to stop him. It felt like it was happening too fast, suddenly. I looked at the clock again. It was half past ten. Becca was lying on her back, and Ryan was kissing her neck, and I wished she would open her eyes so I could see if she was okay. She seemed okay, though. She seemed more than okay.

'There are so many things I haven't said,' I said to Samuel, the words a rush, piling on top of one another. 'So many things I want you to know.'

'Like what?' he asked. His voice was a shrunken version of how it usually sounded.

'Like how much I love you,' I said, trying to keep my own voice steady. 'Like how much I want to be your sister.'

'I know,' he said.

Thomas and Lucy came closer and we huddled. It was the closest we could get to a group hug.

'We can't wait to see you on the other side of it,' Thomas said.

It was true, and it wasn't. The thought of seeing Samuel as a baby, watching him grow the way we'd watched Becca, was wonderful, of course it was, but it was sad, too. We wouldn't be able to communicate with him, to ask his opinion on things.

And before we even got to see him again, we had to wait for nine months.

'Save a space for us,' Lucy said, and we all laughed.

And when I turned back to Becca, she was mostly undressed, on that bed. Her skin was pale and her hair was fanned out behind her. Ryan was on top of her and her hands were running up and down the length of his back. And then, Samuel was gone. Where he'd been, there was only space. Only air.

'Are you okay?' Ryan asked in a whisper.

'Yes.'

He held her close but after a minute or two, she sat up and started putting her clothes back on. Ryan looked at her with a question in his eyes.

'Someone could come in,' she said.

Once they were dressed, their clothes a little crumpled, they lay facing one another, propped up on their elbows.

'Was it your first time?' Ryan asked.

Becca nodded, avoiding his eye.

'It's okay,' he said, picking up her hand from where it lay on the bed between them and folding her fingers inside his.

'I think I'm going to go home,' she said.

'Want me to walk you?' I was glad that he'd offered that.

Becca considered this and then shook her head. I thought she was probably imagining her mum or her dad looking out of the window to see this man bringing her home. The worry it would cause. And the fact that she didn't say yes to it, to spite them, made me think she was going to be all right. Things would always be difficult with her mum, I was pretty sure of that. It was impossible to say what impact Becca having a baby would have on their relationship. For now, all I knew was that Liz was going to move out and there was really no unsaying what she'd said that afternoon. But Becca had her dad, and he adored her. And now she had Samuel, too. She didn't know it, but inside her, he would soon start to grow.

Ryan kissed her and gave her his number, and Becca walked down the stairs and out into the dark, starry night. She was ten minutes from home, and the streets were deserted. It wasn't until she was back at home that she took her phone from her pocket and looked at the message that had come through earlier, when she was lying on the bed with Ryan. It was from Anthony. It said:

> I'm so sorry, Becca Valentine. I got into an accident in Mum's car and my parents were raging. Will you give me another chance?

5

NOVEMBER 2021

We watched Becca do the test, knowing what the result would be. It felt strange, to see a sign that Samuel was there, with her, even though she couldn't feel him yet. I looked at those blue lines and I thought of him curled up tight. Of course, he wasn't curled up yet, he was just a group of cells, dividing and dividing. Her period was a week late. She hadn't told a soul.

When she left the bathroom with the test wrapped up in toilet paper and shoved into the pocket of her jeans, she went into her bedroom and took out her phone. I was expecting her to call Ellie. So I was surprised to hear her say Ryan's name. She'd seen Ryan a couple of times since it had happened. They hadn't had sex again. There hadn't really been an opportunity. That Saturday afternoon, she asked if she could go to his flat, and he laughed and said yes. And I thought about what he was expecting, and how far away it was from what was actually going to happen. I hoped he would be kind.

Twenty minutes later, he opened the door and pulled Becca inside. She was dressed casually, in jogging bottoms and an old T-shirt, a denim jacket that didn't look like it was giving her much protection from the cold. He'd never seen her like that. No makeup, her hair scraped into a ponytail. He stood back from her, looked at her with his nose a little wrinkled, confused. As if wondering what had happened to her. He had no idea.

'I know I look a mess,' she said.

She left a gap for him to disagree, and he took a little too long to do it.

'No, you look fine.'

I noticed Thomas and Lucy sharing a look. They wanted Ryan out of her life, regardless of what that meant for me. But I knew something they didn't. I knew how to make things happen. I'd been practising hard, since Samuel went. It seemed important now, that I used what he'd taught me. And the night before, for the first time, I'd had something to show for it.

Becca had been doing homework in her room. *Go downstairs*, I'd thought. *Go downstairs. Go downstairs.* I'd kept repeating it, over and over. And then, after a good couple of minutes, she'd stood up, left the room. Gone downstairs.

'Did you do that?' Lucy had asked, incredulous.

'I did!'

Becca had gone into the kitchen, where her dad was sitting, writing a shopping list.

'Hi,' he'd said.

'Hi,' Becca had said, a look of confusion on her face.

'What is it?'

'Nothing, I just... I came down here for something and now I can't remember what it was.'

Her dad had laughed. 'I do that sometimes.'

'Hold on,' Thomas had said. 'Eliza, are you trying to tell us you communicated with her somehow, and got her to go downstairs?'

'Yes!' I'd said.

'Bullshit,' Lucy had sneered. And then, after a pause, 'Do it again.'

'It's pretty exhausting, but I'll try.'

We'd all been silent. Becca had taken a can of Diet Coke from the fridge.

Drop it, I'd thought. *Drop it. Drop it. Drop it. Drop it.* But she hadn't. We'd heard the crack and fizz of it opening, and I'd wondered, as I always did, what it tasted like.

'I don't think I can,' I'd said, and Lucy had made a noise that was a sort of scoff.

So they didn't believe me, but that was fine. I knew.

* * *

Ryan's flat was cramped and messy. Jeans on the floor in the bedroom. The sink in the tiny kitchen full of dirty plates and cups. Magazines piled up on the floor by the sofa.

Ryan led her through to the living room.

'I'm pregnant,' Becca said. Her voice was strong, louder than it needed to be. I wondered whether she'd practised inside her head, and it had come out differently to how she'd expected.

Ryan had moved closer to the window, but he whipped around at her words. 'What?'

Don't make her say it again, I wished. It must have been hard enough to say it at all.

'I think you heard,' she said.

I was surprised at her strength. Perhaps the knowledge that she was about to become a mother had changed her. Perhaps it had given her clarity.

'It was one time,' Ryan said. He held his hands up, as if he was trying to physically deny his involvement. 'No one gets pregnant after one time.'

'I did, though,' Becca said. She sat down on the sofa without being asked. She crossed her legs. 'Look, I know it's a shock. It was a shock for me. But it's true.'

Ryan stood very still for a moment, and then he started to pace like an animal. 'This can't be happening.'

He sounded angry and I wanted her to leave but I knew she wouldn't.

'Ryan, sit down. It isn't anyone's fault. Let's talk about this.'

It's his fault, I thought. He was older and he should have used a condom. He should have at least *offered* to use one. And then I thought about Samuel, and I was glad he hadn't. Now she just had to get through this, decide what she was going to do. I was braced for Ryan to suggest an abortion; I was braced for her to agree. I had to be. But I truly believed that that wasn't what she wanted. If it was, why would she have come to him at all? She could have talked to her dad and to Ellie and done what needed to be done. The fact that she'd gone to Ryan suggested, to me, that she wanted to make this work.

He sat down at the very edge of the sofa, as if he wasn't quite prepared to commit to that course of action. He rested his elbows on his knees and placed his head in his hands.

I thought again of Samuel, of the fact that these were his parents, and they barely knew each other and they certainly didn't know him. And worst of all, they had no idea whether they wanted him at all. It was overwhelming. Would it be like this for all of us? We wouldn't know, of course, because by the time people were reacting to the pregnancy, we would no longer be watching. I hoped it wouldn't always be like this. All this heavy silence, these sad looks. And I was glad then, that Samuel wasn't here to see it.

It had been a while since either of them had spoken, and Becca looked like she was determined not to crack first. When Ryan did speak, it seemed like he'd moved on from denial and into a host of justifications.

'I'm not ready for this,' Ryan said. There was a pause, which Becca didn't fill. 'I mean, come on. I can barely afford this place, and I'm too young. I'm twenty-two!'

Ryan was a car salesman. We'd learned that the second time they met. I could imagine him as one. He had that charm, that way of making you feel like he only cared about what you were saying.

Becca just sat there while he went on, telling her things she already knew and not really offering any kind of a suggestion or solution, as if she understood that he needed to get all of this off his chest, and then they would be able to have a proper conversation.

'It was one time,' Ryan said again, as if someone had questioned that. He got up and strode over to the kitchen. He pulled a can of beer from the fridge, opened it with a fizz and took a long swig. 'Do you want anything?' he asked.

Becca shook her head. I saw that there were tears in her eyes, threatening to spill, and I knew that that tiny act of kindness, that offer of a drink, had undone her. She'd been ready for his distaste, but not for that. It struck me as the saddest thing in the world.

When he sat down again, he moved closer to her and reached for her hand. 'What are you going to do?' he asked.

That 'you' hung heavy in the room. They weren't in this together. They weren't going to get through it as a team, as a unit.

'I don't know,' Becca whispered. 'I only just found out. I don't know.'

Ryan looked at her, and I saw him realising what I'd suspected. She might not be saying it, but she wanted to have this baby.

'I'm not ready for this,' he said again.

'There's no being ready for this,' Becca said, shaking her head. 'Especially not like this, when you've only just met me, and you never thought it could happen.'

'You could have a termination,' he said, and something in his voice gave him away. He was trying to sound carefree, as if he was talking about nothing more important than an unwanted plant or a goldfish, but there was a tiny shake to his voice. I wondered whether Becca had noticed it.

Becca let herself cry, then. The tears spilled and fell, and when Ryan saw, he pulled her into his chest and gave her a hug. And it was reminiscent of the first time they'd met, when he'd held her in the garden at that party. But everything had changed.

'It's the only way out that I can see,' he said. 'I don't know what else to do.'

'I don't know either,' Becca said.

They were silent for a few minutes. When the embrace came to a natural end, they just sat there, next to one another, a picture of unhappiness.

'My mum's a nurse,' Ryan said eventually. 'I can talk to her about it. She'll be able to talk us through the options.'

I wondered what had made him switch from 'you' to 'us'. I could see that Becca had noticed it and was glad. She nodded, agreeing. It was a sort of plan, and it was better than nothing.

After that, it seemed like there wasn't anything else for her to do but leave. When she said, into the silence between them, that she had to get back, his expression was one of relief. I thought about him waiting for her to arrive, planning to kiss her in the hallway and lead her into his bedroom where they'd spend the afternoon discovering each other's bodies, with no idea of what was about to happen to him.

At the door, he pulled her into another hug. He didn't kiss her. It was almost impossible to think that they'd been intimate enough with each other to create a baby, in the cool light of that November afternoon.

'I'll call, once I've spoken to my mum,' Ryan said. 'Tomorrow, probably.'

Becca nodded. She looked tired. She began to walk away. She walked slowly, as if she was expecting him to call her back and offer something different, but he didn't, and when she got to the end of the road, and turned back, his door was closed.

She didn't go home. Ellie's house was a ten-minute walk from Ryan's flat, and she went there.

'Can you imagine having to break the news over and over again?' Lucy asked. 'When it's not exactly good news, I mean.'

I wanted to say that it was good news, that it was Samuel, but of course I knew what she meant.

'Ellie will be kind,' I said, hoping that was true.

When Becca got to Ellie's, she shivered on the doorstep in her thin denim jacket. Ellie opened the door and ushered her inside and up the stairs. As soon as Ellie's bedroom door was closed, Becca told her, and Ellie's mouth hung open in shock. The day after it had happened, Becca had told Ellie they'd had sex, but she hadn't gone into detail the way they usually did with one another. And when we'd seen Becca start to worry about her period being late, we'd kept expecting her to talk to Ellie about it, but she hadn't. Becca sunk onto the bed. She looked stunned, as if she'd only just realised the enormity of this thing that was happening to her.

'I thought you used something,' Ellie said, and I could tell from the years of conversations between the two of them that she was trying to keep her voice level. 'Why didn't you use something?'

Becca shrugged her shoulders, as if to say she was tired of talking about it already. It was too late now, wasn't it, so what was the point of asking? 'I don't know,' she said. 'I thought he would take care of it? I didn't really think.'

'But afterwards,' Ellie persisted, her voice a little higher, verging on screechy. 'Didn't you think about getting the morning after pill?'

Becca shook her head. 'I was a mess. It was the weekend my mum was moving out, Anthony had stood me up. I just, sort of, put it out of my mind.'

This isn't what she needs, I thought. She doesn't need to be told about all the little mistakes she's made. This is where she is, and she needs a friend to help her, to help guide her. And it was as if Ellie had heard my thoughts, because she changed tack, then. She could see how defeated Becca looked.

'I'm sorry,' she said. 'Ignore me. It's a shock, that's all. How do you feel?'

Finally, I thought. The right question.

'As in, physically? Or mentally?' Becca asked.

'Both.'

'I'm a bit queasy, have been for a few days. Can't face breakfast. I should have known. Other than that, I don't know. I just told Ryan. He wants me to have an abortion.'

'Did he say that?' Ellie asked, looking shocked.

'Pretty much. I knew he wouldn't exactly be pleased, but I thought he might consider the other option.'

'What do you want?'

'I want to not be pregnant without having to do anything about it,' Becca said.

And Ellie said nothing, because there was nothing to say. When she went down to the kitchen to make cups of tea, Becca stood and moved about the room, taking books from the bookcase and looking at the posters on Ellie's wall, all of which she'd seen a hundred times. I thought she was probably just trying to think about anything else for a minute or two. Ellie returned with two mugs and handed one to Becca, then she pulled two Penguin biscuits out of the pocket of her jeans and they unwrapped them and ate and drank in comfortable silence.

'How are things with Luke?' Becca asked after a while.

Ellie was seeing Anthony's friend Luke. It had started slowly, after the party at Ellie's house. Luke hadn't gone to university. He was working behind a bar, trying to decide what to do next.

'Fine. Good, I think. He still talks about how much Anthony likes you.'

Becca had never replied to Anthony's message, about giving him another chance. He'd sent her several more, telling her how sorry he was. I thought that if she hadn't gone to that party and met Ryan, she would probably have accepted his apology eventually. But it was too late, by the time she saw his message. It was done.

Becca put her head in her hands. 'This wouldn't be happening if I'd gone out with him instead.'

'You don't know that,' Ellie said.

But she did, I thought. If she was seeing Anthony, it would be a slower, calmer thing altogether. Gentler. They probably wouldn't have started sleeping together. I forced myself to look straight ahead, unwilling to see the looks on Lucy's and Thomas's faces.

'Did I make a mistake?' Becca asked.

Ellie furrowed her brow, confused.

'Did I choose the wrong one? I liked Anthony so much, and I thought it was going to happen, but then he let me down on a night when I really needed someone and then I met Ryan and he just seemed so—'

'Exciting?' Ellie offered.

'I guess so. Older, more experienced. But now this has happened, and I wonder whether I just got it all wrong.'

Ellie's eyes glazed over and I thought she was probably imagining if this was her. She and Luke hadn't slept together yet, but they would before long. I could almost see her thinking that it could have been her. That she could have been the one with this terrible burden to carry. I wished I could let her know that she didn't have to worry. We'd questioned her Almosts years ago about their conception dates, and they were years down the line. I looked across then, at her first Almost, Henry. He smiled shyly at me. I liked him. Over the years, we'd talked about all sorts of things. Of her five Almosts, I liked him the most, could imagine being friends with him on the other side. But we never would be. Even if we both made it, I would be twelve by the time he was born.

'It's strange, isn't it,' Ellie said, 'that people try for years to get pregnant, and other people get pregnant accidentally, after one time. It can be the best or the worst thing that could happen.'

Becca scrunched up her nose. 'What's your point? That I should give the baby to someone who wants one?'

'No, I wasn't thinking that. I don't know what I was thinking, really. It just seems strange. But I suppose that is one of the things you could do. Adoption.'

'I'd have to go through it all, though, wouldn't I? The pregnancy and all the stares at school and then the birth, and after all that, I'd have nothing to show for it. And everyone would know. I'd be that girl who got pregnant at school and then gave her baby away. You can't win, can you, as a girl? No one will say anything about Ryan, but I'll be called a slut whether I have an abortion or have the baby. You can't win.'

I had never seen her looking so sad. She folded the red wrapper of the chocolate biscuit up into a tiny square and threw it in the bin that sat beneath Ellie's desk. They were sitting on the floor with their backs against the side of Ellie's bed.

'I wish we could go back to being seven,' Becca said, after a pause. 'When we used to play with My Little Ponies and Barbies in this room. We were so desperate to grow up, weren't we?'

'We were,' Ellie agreed.

'And now here we are. All grown up, and it's shit.'

'Becca,' Ellie said tentatively. 'If you want to keep the baby, you know that's okay, don't you?'

Becca met her friend's gaze. She looked surprised. But she shouldn't have been. Ellie had known her forever, and she could read her almost as well as we could. 'Thank you,' she said. 'I think I needed someone to say that.'

Ellie reached out one arm and pulled Becca a little closer to her, wrapped her arm around her friend's neck. Becca tilted her head to one side and rested it on Ellie's shoulder, and they sat there like that, each a comfort to the other.

6

NOVEMBER 2021

When Ryan called the next day, it wasn't what any of us expected. We had to get really close to Becca to hear his words over the phone line.

'I'm sorry for how I reacted,' he said. 'I was just... I wasn't expecting it.'

'Neither was I,' Becca said, almost a whisper.

'No, of course, and I should have handled it differently. Can we start again?'

'What does he mean?' I asked aloud.

Lucy and Thomas stayed silent.

'What do you mean?' Becca asked.

There was a pause and we heard Ryan sigh. 'I spoke to my mum. She said that if you – if we – want to have an abortion, she's happy to talk us through it. But she said that we should talk about the other options, too, and she's right. I wasn't in the right frame of mind yesterday, but I've had time to think about it now. Would it really be the worst thing, having a baby together?'

Becca smiled, and you could hear it in her voice. 'I don't think so.'

'Well then, let's talk about it. Can you come over?'

We all looked at one another after she ended the call. It was an about turn none of us had seen coming, and Lucy was trying to hide her anger about it for my sake, and I was trying to hide my excitement for hers. I looked at Thomas, trying to gauge his view, but he was hard to read. Becca, at least, seemed happy. The happiest we'd seen her since she'd taken that test. When her dad asked where she was going as she pulled her boots on, I remembered that she still had to break the news to him, if they decided to keep it. I wondered whether she'd tell her mother. Becca hadn't seen her since she'd left, and her dad hadn't tried to push it.

'Just going to Ryan's for a bit,' Becca said.

Her dad nodded. 'And am I ever going to get to meet this mysterious Ryan?'

'I think so,' Becca said. 'I'm pretty sure you will.'

That afternoon, they talked about their options. Abortion, adoption, baby. It was pretty clear early on that Becca wanted to keep it, and Ryan seemed surprisingly open to that. It went dark as they talked, and when they heard the first firework, Becca jumped.

'Bonfire Night,' Ryan said.

'I'd completely forgotten.'

I thought about how much she'd loved Halloween and Bonfire Night when she was a little girl, how her dad had bought her sparklers to hold in the garden and made hot dogs, and then when she was a bit older they'd gone to the organised bonfire and firework display in town. This was the first year they hadn't done anything, and the fact that Becca had forgotten about it showed how distracted she'd been. Or that she'd grown up, I supposed. She stood up and went to the patio door and watched as one firework after another lit up the sky. Ryan came and stood behind her, his arms draped around her neck. And Becca smiled, and it seemed genuine. It seemed true.

By the time they parted, it was decided. Becca would finish her A levels and then have the baby. They would move into Ryan's flat. They even talked about later, how Becca might go to university after another year or two. Ryan said that Becca could still do whatever she wanted to do, and she nodded as if she believed him, or almost did. She walked home with all the worry gone from her face, despite the fact that they'd agreed she would break the news to her parents that evening.

I was relieved, too. I'd thought we were going to lose him again. Samuel. And I would have understood it, I really would. Becca was so young, and the relationship was new, and there were a thousand good reasons not to bring a baby into it. But I was glad they were. I was over the moon that they were.

It was hard to share the relief. Lucy and Thomas would never have said it, I don't think, because they knew how I felt about Samuel, and they loved him too. But I think they'd hung their hopes on an abortion. An abortion, followed by a break-up, followed by a happy ever after with their father, Anthony. This was the first spanner in the works. And if I was going to have my way, it wouldn't be the last.

* * *

Becca got her parents together to tell them. She must have felt she owed it to her mum to involve her in something big like this. I didn't think she did. But I was curious to see her, all the same. Becca answered the door to her and ushered her into the house, and I saw how strange it was for both of them, now that this was no longer their shared home. Liz had done something to her hair, had a different colour put through it, and she was wearing more makeup than she usually did. Becca didn't comment on any of it, though I'm sure she noticed. There were bigger things on her mind.

Dave was in the kitchen. It was the first time he'd seen her too, and everyone shuffled around a bit uncomfortably while Dave made them all a drink. And then they sat down around the table where they'd eaten countless meals. All those sandwiches and bowls of soup, those dishes of spaghetti Bolognese. If I squinted, I could see Becca as a little girl, flanked by her parents. And then I looked at her again, saw her for what she was. A scared and pregnant teenage girl.

'Is it something to do with Ryan?' her dad asked.

'Who's Ryan?' That came from her mum. If she felt guilty for not knowing, she didn't show it.

'He's my boyfriend,' Becca said, and I saw Dave's head lift at the word, his expression change slightly. 'Yes, it's to do with Ryan. And you're not going to like it.'

Dave inhaled sharply and Liz leaned forward a bit, as if wanting to somehow hear the news a little earlier.

'I'm pregnant,' Becca said. 'We're going to have the baby, and I'm going to move in with him.'

It was a lot, all at once. She must have thought it was better to just get it over with. Her mum looked shell-shocked; her dad, angry.

'You're seventeen years old!' he said. Almost a shout.

'Why do people keep saying that? Do you think I don't know that?'

'Becca, you've done some stupid things over the years, but this is worse than I could have possibly imagined.'

'Really, Dad? Worse than you could have imagined? Worse than me being in trouble with the police, or getting addicted to drugs, or punching someone in the face? Seriously?'

Her dad was on his feet, pacing. But it wasn't a large room and he stopped after he'd crossed it a couple of times.

'What about you, Mum? What do you think?' Becca looked at her mum hopefully, searching for support. It was all wrong, this. Her dad was the one who I would have expected to stand by her.

'He'll calm down,' Lucy said, as if she'd known what I'd been thinking. 'He always does.'

I thought about times when Becca had made him angry. The night she'd stayed out two hours later than they'd agreed, come home drunk. And earlier, the time when Becca and Ellie had been caught stealing sweets from the corner shop. When, as a child, she'd stepped out into the road without looking and a car had had to brake sharply. When she was little, it had all felt the same. But looking back, I could see clearly that sometimes it wasn't about her having done something he perceived as wrong, but about her being unsafe or potentially going down the wrong path, in the wrong direction. He tended to blow up like this, and then talk it all through with her later. So many times, they'd had late-night chats on the sofa after arguments like this. But this time felt different, because it was such a big thing. Another life.

'It's a shock,' her mum said, then. 'It's not what we wanted for you. You have all your life to have a family. Why now? And this Ryan, he can only have been on the scene for such a short time. What makes you think he's the right one for you?'

Becca sank down a little lower in her chair. 'It's not about picking and choosing. Is this one right, or this one? This has happened, and we're dealing with it. I know we haven't been together long, and we didn't plan to have a baby, but it's happening.'

'But there are options, Becca,' her dad cut in. 'I know it's not ideal, but you could make this go away, you could wait a few years.'

'I know that,' Becca said. She was starting to cry. 'Don't you think I know that? Don't you think I know how much easier that would be, in so many ways? We could all pretend it never happened and just carry on. But I've thought about it and I just know it isn't what I want. It isn't the right choice for me. You have to trust me on that.'

'Listen, Becca, you don't know what having a baby entails. Your mum and I, we were older, and we'd been together for a few years, and it still hit us like a truck. It's not all happy families—'

Becca snorted. 'Clearly!'

'It's hard work, is all I'm saying. It's really hard work. Not to mention expensive.'

Her mum was nodding, but she hadn't said anything for a while. Becca looked at her, pleading.

'It's your decision,' her mum said.

It was one of those phrases that didn't really mean anything. Obviously it was her decision. Her body, her baby, all that. I was pretty sure that once her mum walked out of the house later, nothing was going to change. I didn't see her helping out and becoming a doting grandmother.

'I don't think there's anything else to say,' Becca said, and she stood up, prepared to leave the room. I wanted to stay, to see what her parents would say to one another, how things would be left between them, but I didn't have that option. I followed Becca up the stairs to her bedroom, hovered in the corner as she lay face-down on her bed and cried. I felt helpless. I wanted to be able to show them all the person they would be gaining from this. I wanted to tell them about him. Tell them that he was worth it, that he would make them all so proud, and happy.

'She's making a mistake,' Thomas said into the quiet.

'Oh, not you too,' I said. I was weary of everyone feeling this way, everyone talking about this new life like it was the worst thing that could have happened. 'It's one thing them saying that, when they don't know him. But how can you?'

'Eliza, I love Samuel,' he said. 'I want him to have a chance, just like you. But this is going to ruin her life. Surely you can see that. She's too young, and Ryan isn't the right guy. It's going to end badly.'

I wanted to say so many things. That we hadn't chosen him for our father, me and Samuel, that it was just the way it was. That it wasn't fair for him to act as though he and Lucy had more of a right to exist, just because their father seemed more solid, more reliable. That we were people too. Or might be. But I didn't say any of them.

Later, Lucy approached me and came close, closer than she usually did. She didn't say that she was sorry, or that she disagreed with what Thomas had said. She didn't say anything. She was just there. I could feel her solidarity, her silent support. And it was enough.

* * *

The next few days were awful. Becca's dad seemed like he was disappointed in her and didn't say a great deal, and she didn't hear anything from her mum. She just spent most of her time at Ryan's flat, where they watched box sets on TV and talked about what it was going to be like, for the three of them. Becca often felt nauseous, and frequently threw up whatever she'd eaten for dinner, and she was tired all the time, morning and night. Ryan rubbed her back, asked if there was anything he could do. And I could see how it must feel to her. All her life, her dad had been this safety net, this comforting presence, full of love. And just when she needed him most, he'd retreated into himself, unhappy with her decisions. And there was Ryan, stepping up, being there. It felt so good to see it. Maybe he was growing into a better man.

When she went to bed, she often lay awake for over an hour, looking up at the ceiling. And I wished I knew what she was thinking about in those moments, wished I could see inside her brain. I hoped she wasn't changing her mind, about having him. I was frightened of everything; her changing her mind, her miscarrying. I didn't feel that I'd be able to truly believe Samuel would be born until it actually happened. There were going to be some tough months ahead.

And then, when a week had passed, Becca's dad turned up at the school gate at the end of the day, and when Becca approached his car, he put his window down and gestured for her to get in. There was a bitter wind. Becca was wearing a big coat, a scarf and gloves, a woolly hat. She leaned on the open window and peered into the car.

'What?' she asked.

She wasn't going to make it easy for him. She never did.

'I want to talk to you,' her dad said. 'Get in, it's freezing.'

'I'm okay walking,' she said, making to stand.

'Becca, I'm sorry, okay? I said some things I shouldn't have. I want to talk it all through with you. I want to help.'

Slowly, she reached for the door handle, then stopped, pulled her glove off with her teeth and then opened the door.

'Do we have hot chocolate at home?' she asked, sliding into the passenger seat and throwing her bag into the back.

Her dad laughed. 'You'll be lucky. We've got tea, though. Always got tea.'

'Tea will have to do, then.'

I felt safe then, somehow. I hated it when Becca and her dad fell out. I could handle arguments between her mum and dad, or between Becca and her mum. But these two, they were the solid foundation our family was built on, and I couldn't bear it when they weren't united.

They didn't say much on the short drive home. Once they were inside, and Becca had peeled off her outer layers and her dad had put the kettle on, he held out his arms and she walked into them. They stood there, quite still, in the kitchen, for a couple of minutes.

'I'm sorry,' he said. 'I've been an idiot.'

'You have a bit,' Becca said. 'But I should have expected it. No one wants to hear their daughter is knocked up at seventeen, right?'

Her dad winced at her words. 'I do so hate being predictable. So, what's the latest thinking?'

Becca pulled away from him and narrowed her eyes. 'Hold on, are you still trying to talk me into an abortion?'

'No, that wasn't what I was trying to do. I just wanted to be sure you'd thought through your options...'

'I have and nothing's changed. I'm having this baby. The timing is pretty good, in a sense. I'll be due just after I've finished my exams.'

'Let's hope it doesn't come early,' her dad said. 'Did I ever tell you that you were early?'

Becca laughed and rolled her eyes. This was her dad's favourite story. He used to tell it when she couldn't sleep, or when they were sitting on the sofa on rainy days, or when she was low and couldn't really say why.

They moved into the living room together. She plopped down on the sofa and he handed her a mug of tea.

'Tell me about me being early,' she said.

'Well, your mum and I thought we were so organised. We'd bought everything for the hospital bag, we'd read all the books, we'd been to all the classes. And no one had said anything about early babies. We'd heard a lot about late babies, especially first babies. How you might try to bring on labour, when you were huge and uncomfortable and forty-one weeks pregnant. But we had five weeks to go and I hadn't even started planning our route to the hospital yet...'

Becca laughed. The story was so familiar, to her and to us, and her dad's routes were an inside family joke. He always worked out at least two, no matter where they were going.

'And then one night, we were watching TV and I was about to suggest going up to bed, and your mum suddenly cried out in pain, and I was so surprised I dropped a cup of tea' – he gestured down at his cup, as though Becca might not be familiar with the term – 'all over my lap, and she said the baby was coming. I told her it was impossible, that it was far too early, and she just looked at me, and I knew she meant business. So I raced around the house shoving all the things we'd bought into the bag and your mum paced up and down the hallway waiting for me to be ready to go, and then I drove her in, and when we got to the ward, the midwife gave your mum a long look, and then me, and asked whether her waters had broken. I'd completely forgotten that I still had tea all over my trousers. It was so embarrassing. And then, just then, her waters did break, right in the middle of the corridor. Someone went rushing off to get a mop and bucket and one of those yellow 'wet floor' signs, and we were taken into this little room and your mum lay down on the bed and twenty minutes later, you were here.'

Becca visibly relaxed as he told the story. They were home to her, those words. And I imagined that she was starting to feel, like I was, that it was all going to be okay. That she would have the support of her parents, and of Ryan, and she would be a mother. Samuel's mother.

'What about Mum?' she asked when he'd finished. 'Do you think she'll be in our lives? Mine and the baby's, I mean? I haven't heard from her since I told you. I hoped she would come around, like you have.'

Her dad shook his head. 'I don't know, Becca. I feel, somehow, like I've never really known her at all. And I know it's hard for you to hear, but I can't help but be relieved that I'm not around her much any more.'

Becca looked pained but didn't say anything.

'There's still time for things to change. People do, sometimes. I waited for it, but then I just couldn't wait any longer. Anyway, whatever happens, you know that I'll be here for both of you. I promise you that.'

It was a moment when I would always have looked at Samuel to make sure he'd heard. I felt the loss of him so acutely. And then I remembered that all of this was about him, in preparation for him. We didn't have him in our world any longer, but it was only because he was getting ready to enter theirs. And that was the aim, wasn't it? That was the goal, always had been. He was right on track.

7

DECEMBER 2021–JUNE 2022

Once everyone had been told, it felt like Becca's pregnancy moved remarkably swiftly. When Christmas came, Becca and Ryan spent the day with her dad and the evening with his parents. It was strange, the first Christmas after the split, and I worried about Dave when they waved and left to go to Ryan's parents'. I hoped he'd put the TV on and eat some of the chocolates Becca had bought for him. I hoped he wouldn't wallow. I kept thinking about the fact that the next year, there would be a baby in the mix, and that would change everything.

On New Year's Eve, Ryan had plans with his friend Carl, so Becca called Ellie. She was going to the pub with Luke and his friends. She invited Becca to come.

'Will Anthony be there?' Becca asked.

'Probably.'

'Do you know whether he's with anyone?'

'I don't think so. But why do you care, Becca? You are pregnant with someone else's baby...'

Becca bit her lip and didn't answer the question.

'She won't go,' Lucy said, and I was surprised. Lucy was

usually so confident and positive about anything to do with Anthony.

She did go. She spent a long time getting ready and when she left the house, she looked shiny and new. Anthony made his way over to her as soon as she arrived at the pub.

'Hi, Becca. Good Christmas?'

'Hi,' she said. 'Yes, it was okay. You?'

'Oh, you know. I feel like I've eaten at least two whole turkeys.'

It was the first time she'd seen him since they'd spent that night together and she'd thought something was starting between them. It seemed like years ago, to me. I wondered how it felt to her.

'Look, I know it's too late, and I've already told you in those messages, but I just really wanted to say, in person, that I'm sorry about that night when I didn't turn up...'

Becca was looking at him but it was hard to know what she was thinking. That had been the night she'd slept with Ryan and her whole life had changed. Perhaps she was contemplating how different things might be now if he hadn't stood her up.

'It doesn't matter now,' she said, batting at the air with her hand as if to dislodge the memory of it.

'No, I suppose not, I just— I feel so terrible about it. I was looking forward to that night so much. It wasn't that I didn't care, I promise. I would hate you to think that I didn't care.'

'Did you hear that I'm pregnant?' Becca asked.

Anthony met her gaze. 'I did.'

I wondered whether he'd made the connection, whether he knew that this had happened that same night, when he'd let her down. Probably not.

'I'm not sure why I came,' she said, looking down at her feet.

'Because it's New Year,' he said, 'and you wanted to spend it with friends. Can I get you a drink?'

And Becca smiled, and nodded, and he bought her a lemonade and they talked about his course and her A levels, and when 'Yesterday' came on the jukebox, they shared a wistful sort of smile.

'Did you know that Paul McCartney woke up with this song in his head, fully formed, and thought he must have heard it somewhere?' Anthony asked.

'No, I didn't know that.'

'Becca, I...'

He didn't finish the sentence, and I saw that there were tears in her eyes, and I thought he was going to close the space between them and hug her, but he didn't. And when the moment had passed, and she had blinked the tears away, she put a hand gently on his arm and then walked away.

At midnight, Ellie was wrapped around Luke and everyone was drunk except Becca. She put her coat on and tried to slip away without anyone seeing. But Anthony noticed, of course. He touched her arm as she went past him and a group of his friends.

'Happy New Year, Becca Valentine.'

They hugged, and I thought for a moment that she was going to kiss him, and I could feel the anticipation coming off Lucy and Thomas in waves, but then she turned away and went out into the crisp winter night.

* * *

Winter gave way to spring, and we watched her grow, watched the concern and pride mixed on the face of her dad, watched the screen at the ultrasound scans for our first glimpses of Samuel on the other side of things.

In April, at seven months pregnant, Becca turned eighteen. All of her friends' eighteenth birthday celebrations had been drunken affairs, held in pubs and clubs. When Ellie asked what Becca wanted to do for hers, she just shrugged. And in the end, Ryan took her out for dinner at an Italian restaurant in town. She joked that it was their first official date, looking down at her huge belly. Ellie gave her a nail colour set and Ryan bought her a top she liked, a non-maternity top for after the baby had come. Like always, her most thoughtful present was from her dad. He'd made her a wooden chest, the size of a small laptop, and carved her full name and date of birth into the lid.

'For your special things,' he said, shrugging, when she unwrapped it.

Becca hugged him really tight. And later, she went through her drawers and dug out a friendship bracelet Ellie had made her in Year Eight, the ticket to her first concert, a notebook she'd written her favourite Beatles lyrics in and some shells she'd collected on a Cornwall beach as a child, and transferred them to the chest. She put something else in and took it out again, and at first I couldn't make out what it was, but then I saw that it was a pressed blue flower. The one Anthony had tucked into her hair that night of Ellie's party. She held it for a moment, twisting the stem, and then she put it back in the drawer where she'd found it and pushed the chest under her bed.

She had a phone call from her mum, too. It was early evening, an hour or so before Ryan was picking her up to take her out for dinner, and she was sitting in the living room watching TV with her dad. When she saw the name on the screen of her phone, she took several rings to decide whether or not to answer it.

'Hello,' she said, all caution. She stood and left the room, went into the kitchen and pulled the door shut behind her.

'Happy birthday, Becca.'

'Where have you been, Mum?'

'You know where I am...'

'I don't mean that. I haven't seen you for months. You can't just come and go when it suits you, like this.'

I was proud of her for this. She didn't always say what she meant, voice what she was feeling. She didn't always tell people when they had hurt her, and make them answer for it.

'I'll do better,' her mum said. 'I've been finding things hard. I lost my job and I'm still adjusting to living on my own.'

I waited for Becca to break in and say that it was her own fault she was living alone. That she'd had a family and she'd thrown them away. But she stayed quiet.

'I'll do better,' her mum repeated.

Becca nodded, as if her mum was in the same room as her, could see her reaction. 'I'd better go, I'm going out in a bit,' she said. And she ended the call and went back to the living room. Her dad looked up at her, his face open, and I thought he probably knew who had been on the phone, but he didn't ask.

We didn't hear Samuel's name until June, when Becca was eating breakfast on the morning of her final A level exam.

'I've been thinking about what to call him,' she said.

'Oh yes?' her dad asked. He was standing at the sink, his hands busy with the dishes. He turned to look at his daughter.

I pricked up my ears. I had longed to see her mouth make the shape of this word, to hear her say it. I was sure she'd fill it with the love we all felt for him.

'I thought it was going to be Oliver,' she said, 'but I've changed my mind. It's Samuel.'

'Oh, it's lovely,' her dad said.

It was lovely, and like a new name in her mouth. Soft and sweet, serious and sincere. Samuel. When she stood to get more orange juice from the fridge, I looked at her belly, at the full roundness of it. It wouldn't be long now. Just a couple of weeks until he was with them. Becca's things were mostly packed in boxes. They'd decided to save the move into Ryan's flat until school was done and the baby was almost there.

At school, Becca sat with Ellie in the common room. The netball girls were all there, Eve and Suzy and Tasha. I remembered that Ellie had said, months ago, that Tasha was pregnant, that she was going to have an abortion. And it was true. Where once she'd had three Almosts, now there were only two. Becca had never been one of these girls, but now that her maternity jeans were pulled up over her rounded belly, and she was wearing the biggest T-shirt she'd been able to find in H&M to accommodate the baby, she was the lowest of the low. This is how it was with teenage girls, it seemed. For Becca's sake, I wanted to wish away these final few days and look to Samuel's arrival. Once he was there, no one could argue that he wasn't the right thing, could they?

'Is Ryan excited?' Ellie asked.

'Yes,' Becca answered, a little too quickly.

But the truth was, Ryan didn't say much about the baby. Becca had chosen the name, and she had found the things they needed and he had paid for them. Sometimes, when they were spending the evening at his flat – the flat that would soon be theirs – he would put his hand on Becca's bump, almost absently, while they watched TV. Was that excitement? It was something. It was all Becca had.

They made their way to the school hall for this last exam. History. I thought of all the assemblies they'd sat through in this cavernous room. The school discos. The PE lessons on wet days. So recently, it seemed, they'd been children. As they filed in, Becca squeezed Ellie's hand.

'Good luck,' she said.

'You too,' Ellie said, her expression nervous.

They made their way to their separate seats, heads down. For the next three hours, Becca wrote as if her baby's life depended on it. She scrawled page after page, going back to check how many questions she was supposed to answer time and again. In the mock exam, she'd written three essays instead of four by mistake, and it had had a big impact on her grade. She'd cried, and her dad had said it was probably a good thing actually, because she would never make that mistake again. That that was what mock exams were for. Since then, she'd put in long hours in her bedroom and she really knew her stuff. I wondered whether she would have worked so hard if it wasn't for Samuel, kicking away inside her, a physical reminder that she needed to succeed in life, that she had someone to keep alive besides herself.

When the bell rang and she stood to leave that hall for the final time, I could tell from the look on her face that she knew she'd done it. She'd done her best, and her best was pretty good. It would be a couple of months before she got the results, but for now, she could be happy with what she'd done. Ellie looked worried when they met outside on the grass.

'I didn't do enough,' she said. 'Why didn't I do enough?'

'Relax,' Becca said. 'It's done now. There's nothing you can do to change it.'

'It's different for you,' Ellie said. 'You know what you're going to be doing after the summer.'

Becca didn't say anything, but I was pretty sure she was annoyed. Just because she was having a baby, it didn't mean that her education didn't matter any more. In a way, it mattered more. Ellie had an offer of a place to study Business and Economics at a university in London, but she had to get two As and a B, and History was her weak spot. Before the pregnancy, Becca had planned to take a year out, at least partly because she hadn't been able to decide what she wanted to study. Sometimes, when she was on her own in her room, she still went to the UCAS website and scrolled up and down a bit, seeming completely overwhelmed.

'Do you still think you'll go to uni at some point?' Ellie asked.

She hadn't broached this subject before. They'd talked a lot about exams, and then the baby coming, but not really about after. About Becca's plans for the rest of her life.

Becca lay back, propping her body up with her elbows. The position made her bump look enormous, and she stared at it as she spoke. 'I don't know,' she said. 'I think I'll take a year, see how I get on, decide later.'

Ellie couldn't quite manage a smile, and I could see that she was thinking this might mark the end of their friendship. She'd go round when the baby was born, of course she would. She'd take a cute outfit and have a cuddle and promise to help out, but things would taper off. They'd have so little in common. Ellie would be commuting into London for lectures, and Becca would be stuck at home with a new baby, constantly feeding and going for walks with the pram and all that. There would be so little common ground.

'There's a party at Tasha's later. Do you fancy it?' Ellie asked.

Becca shook her head. 'I can't. I'm a freak show. Honestly, the way people look at me, you'd think none of them had ever had sex.'

It was true. Every party they went to, there were people sneaking off to the bedrooms. All Becca's bump was proof of was that she'd done it too. Why was it so shocking to everyone? Maybe it was the fear of it, I thought. The close-up proof that it really could happen to anyone.

'Will you go?' Becca asked.

Ellie nodded her head almost imperceptibly. 'Probably. It feels like a big deal, finishing. I feel like I need to mark it somehow. Unless you want to do something different, just you and me?'

It was clear that she was hoping Becca would say no to this. And Becca did. I wondered what she really wanted, whether she would have liked to do something special with her best friend if things were different. The chasm that had opened between the two girls yawned a little wider.

'I think I'll go home,' Becca said, and she stood up. 'My dad's making a special dinner.'

They parted ways. Becca didn't look back. But I did. Ellie was watching her friend leave, a confused look that was something like sadness but also like relief on her face.

* * *

'It's funny,' Becca's dad said when she was shrugging off her cardigan after getting home that afternoon. 'I know I see you every day but it's like I forget you're pregnant sometimes, and I'm so surprised when I notice.'

'A good surprise, or a bad one?' Becca asked.

'Well,' her dad said, 'you know I wasn't all that pleased at first. I think you're too young. You know that. But it's happening, isn't it, so there's no point dwelling on all that. And I'm pretty excited about having a baby around again.'

They were in the kitchen by then, and her dad held up the kettle, raised his eyebrows.

'Tea, please,' Becca said. 'Why didn't you and Mum have any more children?'

When Becca was young, she'd often asked for a brother or a sister, and her parents had exchanged loaded looks. I remembered the things Becca couldn't possibly remember, the way her mum had struggled with motherhood, the afternoons she'd spent crying, the times her dad had asked whether they might try again and she'd pushed him away. I was curious about how much he'd reveal, now that they were no longer together.

'You were enough for us,' he said.

Becca wasn't taken in. 'I don't believe you. You were such a great dad. I think you would have wanted to do it again.'

I thought about Liz's other Almosts, Sarah and Charles. A few weeks before Sarah's conception date, Dave had approached Liz about them trying again but she shut it down. Charles's date was a couple of years later and Dave made one last-ditch plea that fell on deaf ears.

Her dad busied himself with adding milk to two mugs. 'I wouldn't have said no,' he responded. 'Your mum wasn't keen.'

Becca leaned back against the kitchen cupboards and blew air out of her cheeks. 'I'm not sure she should have had a child,' she said. 'I think she meant it, you know, when she said she wasn't sure why she'd had me.'

It was true that her mum had never been a natural mother, had always relied on her husband to make the decisions for them. It was like she'd had no innate mothering instincts. Perhaps some people just didn't.

'I think maybe she did too,' her dad said sadly. 'But that isn't about you, it's about her. Try to remember that.'

'I sometimes worry,' Becca said, once her dad had handed her a mug of tea and was standing opposite, blowing on his own. 'She always seemed like she wanted to be somewhere else. What if I'm like that? What if I've inherited that from her?'

'Oh, Becca, you won't be. The very fact that you're already worrying about whether you'll be a good mother shows me that you will be. Does that make sense? Things were tough for your mum. Our marriage wasn't perfect, and she was young.'

'But I'm young. And I'm not married – things are still pretty new with Ryan. What if I'm being selfish, having the baby? What if he resents me?'

Her dad sighed and put his mug down, folded his arms across his chest. 'There are so many mistakes you can make, as a parent. You can't possibly avoid them all. And if you worry about them too much, you'll find yourself consumed. And then you won't be a good parent. It's a really tricky business.'

'How did you get it so right?' Becca asked.

Her dad smiled and his face reddened a little. 'I just loved you, Becca. I loved you more than anything else, and everything followed on from that. It's all about making decisions, you know. Every day, every hour, even, you're making one decision after another. But if you base them all on the love you feel, I don't think you can go far wrong.'

Later, when they were sitting at the kitchen table eating pork chops, her dad asked how she felt the exams had gone.

'I know you might feel that none of it matters much now,

with the baby coming and everything. But those qualifications will come in handy later on, I promise you.'

'I know that. It made me work harder, if anything.'

'And how are things with Ryan?' her dad asked.

It was obvious that he'd had to work up to this. I could tell by the look on his face that he was hiding his true feelings about Ryan and the whole situation. I'm sure Becca could too.

'It's good, I think. I mean, it's not what either of us expected, or planned. But we're going to be okay.'

Her dad nodded, but I could see he wasn't sure. I was glad that he left it there, didn't argue.

A little later, they watched an old sitcom repeat on TV. It was something they'd watched together years before, and they laughed in all the same places as one another, and I wondered whether they noticed.

'The baby's kicking,' Becca said. She reached across and grabbed his hand, put it firmly on her bump. 'Can you feel it?'

He shook his head in amazement. 'It takes my breath away.'

They were silent, and the programme finished, and neither of them changed the channel. Something else came on, something about cruise ships. I waited for one or the other of them to say they were going up to bed.

'I'm scared, Dad,' Becca said.

And my head spun around to look at her just as his did.

'Scared of what?'

'Of the birth, of not being able to handle the pain. And then of being a mum. Of not knowing how. I'll be living with Ryan, and it will be my first time away from home and we're still getting to know each other, and suddenly there'll be another person in the mix and I'm just afraid that maybe it will all be too much.'

Lucy and Thomas were beside me. I could sense them.

'I hate this,' I said. 'I hate that she's already half-regretting Samuel, and he's not even there yet.'

'It'll be okay,' Thomas said. He didn't sound sure.

'It'll be okay,' Becca's dad said. But he *did* sound sure. 'You know, I'm here, and I'm not going anywhere. I didn't know much about being a dad before you came along, and I muddled through. I'll help you, Becca. You just have to let me.'

'Okay,' she said, and she smiled a half smile. 'I think I'm going to go to bed.' She pushed herself up off the sofa. At the door, she turned back. 'Thank you. Sometimes I can't sleep and I can feel him kicking and I just worry about where we're going to be in five years' time, or ten years. It all feels so uncertain, other than the fact that I'm going to have him.'

'You'll have me, too,' her dad said.

'I know.'

She lay in bed that night looking at her phone for a long time. She sent Ellie a message asking how the party was but didn't get a reply. And then she went to the messages that had gone back and forth between her and Anthony. Read them through. When she got to the end, her finger hovered over the screen and it looked like she was going to start typing something, but then she put the phone down on the floor beside her bed and closed her eyes.

8

JUNE 2022

When the contractions started, a week before Becca's due date, only I was with her. It was late, or early, somewhere in those hours between midnight and morning, when she sat up in bed with no warning. I'd been waiting in the corner of the room, knowing it could happen at any time, and desperate to see Samuel. I called Lucy's and Thomas's names into the darkness, and in a moment they were beside me, and we watched as Becca moved her hands from her belly to her back, as if unsure where the pain was coming from.

Pain was something that intrigued us. We couldn't imagine it. We'd heard them talking about sharp or dull pain, pain that spreads and pain that makes you shout out. Our own bodies were useless and we felt nothing. And I longed for those sensations, even the unpleasant ones.

'She wanted to move in with Ryan before he came,' Lucy said.

It was true, but every time she'd asked Ryan to help with her things, he'd been too busy. Making excuses? Was there a chance he was going to back out of being Samuel's father?

Becca stayed in her bedroom for the next couple of hours, and each time she clutched at herself, I wished I could feel some of the pain for her. Partly because I loved her, and I wanted to help, but partly because I was so ready to feel.

Those hours alone with her were special, because we knew that Samuel was on his way. I longed to see his eyes, to hear his voice, if only as a cry. But it became clear, gradually, that the pain was becoming too much, and just before dawn, Becca went to her dad's bedroom and knocked on the door.

We heard her dad inviting her in, his voice thick with sleep. Becca entered the room and stood at the foot of his bed. And when the pain overtook her once more, she gripped the footboard.

'The baby's coming,' she said.

It didn't really need to be said. Her dad was already out of bed and pulling on his clothes.

'Can you get yourself dressed?' he asked.

Becca nodded but didn't move.

'Come on, the quicker we get you there, the better. You'll be in good hands.'

Still, Becca didn't move. The contraction had subsided, but still she clung to the end of her dad's bed. A single tear tracked down the left side of her face.

'Do you think Mum will come, if we call her?' she asked.

Her dad was pulling a jumper out of a drawer when Becca said this.

'I'll call her. You just get yourself ready to go. You've got your bag ready, yes?'

Becca's hospital bag had been packed and in the corner of her bedroom for a month. She nodded, left the room.

Becca got dressed. She called Ryan. He said, sleepily, that he would meet them there, and I hoped fervently that he wouldn't roll over and go back to sleep. He was a heavy sleeper. He'd taken ages to answer the phone. *She needs you*, I said, over and over. I was right beside her. I didn't think it would change anything, but I hoped anyway.

They didn't say much on the drive to the hospital. Becca had a couple of contractions on the journey, and it seemed like she had to concentrate when she was having them, to focus somehow to get through it. Her dad drove quickly but carefully, and it wasn't long before he was pulling into a space in the hospital car park. The sun was rising and the sky was pink and it looked like it was on fire, and I wondered whether either of them had noticed it. It was a beautiful day to be born. Becca's dad helped her out of the car and to the door. Daughter leaning on father. Father taking the strain.

They were assigned a midwife and a room after Becca had been examined and found to be in active labour. The midwife's name was Jessica. She was young; no more than twenty-six or twenty-seven. She told them that she'd birthed over a hundred babies. It was almost defensive, the way this information was given, and I wondered whether people had made jokes about her age before, referred to her as a student or newly qualified. She had sparkling brown eyes and I trusted her, and I hoped that Becca did too. I looked around for her Almosts, as I always did when Becca met a new woman. There were two, peering out from behind Jessica. Two girls.

'We're twins,' one of them said. 'Ava and Edith.'

I smiled. 'What's your date?'

'Ninth of September 2024,' they answered in unison.

'That's just a few days before mine!'

'But we don't think she's met our dad yet,' Ava said, sounding sad.

'You'd know,' I said. 'You just... know.'

'Are they married, your parents?' Edith asked.

'No,' I said. I wasn't sure how to explain it.

'The guy she's with now, he's not Thomas's and mine,' Lucy said, indicating Thomas with a tilt of her head. 'He's not *our* dad. Just Samuel and Eliza's. It's complicated.'

'Who's being born today?' Edith asked, skirting around the subject of fathers.

'Samuel,' I said.

I tried to inject all my love into his name, to show them, without telling them, that he was the most important person in the world to me, that these next few hours were critical.

'She'll keep him safe,' Ava said. 'Our mum. She's the best.'

We all looked over at her. She was talking to Becca, trying to put her at ease. She was kind, and she cared. Becca and Samuel couldn't have been in better hands.

'Is the dad...?' Jessica asked.

'On his way,' Becca said.

By this time, Becca was struggling with the pain. Jessica arranged for her to have gas and air, and the panic in the room subsided for a while. There followed an hour or two of steady progress; strong contractions mixed with ever shorter rest periods, during which Becca's dad tried to keep her spirits up and engage her in conversation. And all that time, Ryan didn't arrive. Between contractions, Becca asked to look at her phone. She sent him a couple of messages, but there was no response.

'You know,' her dad said, 'if he lets you down today, and you want to change your mind about moving in...'

'He's on his way,' Becca said, her voice all steel.

And he was, it turned out. Just when we'd all stopped expecting him, Ryan burst into the room, looking dishevelled.

'I'm sorry,' he said, out of breath. 'It took me ages to park and then I couldn't find the right bit of the hospital. How are you doing?'

Becca looked up at him, really focused on his eyes. 'I needed you here,' she said. She looked like she was about to cry.

'And I'm here.'

'I'll go,' Becca's dad said, 'now Ryan's here. I'll call your mum, find out where she is.'

There was silence in the room for a minute or two, but the next contraction broke it. Ryan looked horrified as it took hold of Becca, moving further into the room and grabbing her hand.

And when the contraction was over, Jessica spoke. 'Have you settled on a name?' she asked.

'Samuel,' Becca said. She looked tired. Her face was pale, with two pink spots at her cheeks. She was ready for this to be over. We all were.

'That's lovely,' Jessica said, her eyes flashing joy.

She loved her job. You could tell.

'I don't think I can do it,' Becca said, then.

I watched Jessica's face for any tell-tale signs that she was worried, but there were none.

'I know you feel that way, Becca. But the good news is, that means he's nearly here. All women feel like giving up just before it all happens. I've seen it over and over again. Just a few more contractions and you'll have your baby, I promise.'

Becca didn't answer but I could see the determination in the set of her face. She could do this. She was going to do it. She might have messed things up by ending up here at the age of eighteen, but she was going to make the best of it. I felt proud, as if I were the parent and she was the child. For the next handful of contractions, it was as if she was possessed. I saw the way she pushed, harder than before, saw the encouraging look on Jessica's face, the admiration in Ryan's. It was really happening.

A little before five in the afternoon, Becca let out a sound I'd never heard from her. It was a kind of roar, part-terror, all-power, and the head emerged, and Jessica cradled it in her hands. I looked at him, at Samuel, ready to treasure my first glimpse of him, but he was covered in blood and I couldn't make him out properly. I was impatient then, after nine months of missing him, to have him back.

'That's it!' Jessica shouted. 'That's the head, Becca. That's wonderful. Now breathe and wait for the next one to come.'

Lucy and Thomas were beside me, our bodies close together. If we'd been like them, if we'd been alive, we would have been touching. We didn't crowd in like that often, but this was different from any other moment we'd shared. I looked from Samuel's face to Becca's, willed her to find the strength to expel him with the next contraction. And she did. Like a warrior woman, and not at all like a scared, eighteen-year-old girl, she pushed with a might that I could almost feel, and his little body slithered out of hers, and he was in Jessica's arms, and Becca was crying with the relief of it all.

Jessica rubbed him and wrapped him up and then handed him to his mum to hold. Becca appeared poised and beautiful, even as she was passing the placenta and her blood-spattered legs were shaking.

'Look at him,' she said, talking to Ryan.

And we all did. We drank him in. A full head of slick, dark hair, a tiny, pouting mouth that was already rooting for milk, and those eyes. Big, so dark they were almost black, and full to the brim of wisdom and living. Surely they would see that he wasn't brand new.

'He's different from how I remember him, somehow,' Lucy said.

Thomas and I agreed. He was different, but very definitely him. Things were restored, now that he was with them.

Ryan wiped at his eyes with the cuff of his sweatshirt. 'Wow,' he said. 'That was incredible.'

Her dad came in after the midwife told him the news. He was beaming and proud. He held Samuel, who looked smaller in his big arms, and kissed his head and each of his fingers.

'Where's Mum?' Becca asked.

'She's... on her way. Won't be long now.'

Becca had a sleep, and Ryan went to the café to get something to eat, and her dad looked after his grandson. They sat in a comfy chair by the window and her dad talked softly, pointing towards the flat Samuel would live in, his own house, the school Becca had attended.

When Becca woke, she looked disoriented. I wondered whether she'd dreamed, whether she was now having to unpick what was real and what wasn't. I hoped she remembered that Samuel was real, that he was hers. Her dad must have heard her moving in the bed, because he turned with a smile, Samuel fast asleep in his arms.

'Look what you did,' he said.

Becca flashed him a smile, but she seemed almost embarrassed by this praise. 'Can I have him?' she asked.

'Of course.' He brought Samuel over and passed him to her, carefully.

'You know, things will never be quite the same now,' he said. 'And sometimes, they'll seem worse. Definitely harder. But I can assure you, they're better. Worth more. But there's no doubt, it's tough. Remember I'm here for you.'

Becca blinked away tears and nodded. 'I'm going to make you proud,' she said.

Her dad shook his head. 'You've already done that,' he said. 'Make him proud, now.'

* * *

By the time her mum appeared, it seemed like she'd missed everything.

'I'm sorry,' she said. 'I was caught up with something. I came as soon as I could.'

'What could be more important?' I asked.

'It doesn't matter, really, does it?' Thomas asked. 'She should have been here, and she wasn't. Story of Becca's life.'

She'd only been there for half an hour, had only just had a cuddle with her grandson, when visitors were asked to go home and Becca was moved from her private room to a ward. Samuel was put in a strange plastic cot on wheels and placed next to her bed. There were three other women lying on beds in the room, and beside each of them, one of these cots, a sleeping or stretching baby inside.

'Will you be okay?' Ryan asked.

'I'll have to be,' Becca said.

He leaned down to kiss her, and then her parents did the same, and they all left together – an odd threesome. Becca watched their backs as they disappeared. It was impossible to know what she was thinking. Whether she was wondering how she was going to cope with all of this, or wishing that Ryan could have stayed, or thinking about what took him and her mum so long to get there that morning. When they were out of sight, she lay back on the bed, her face level with Samuel's. And they looked at each other, eyes wide.

9

AUGUST 2022

Those early weeks were tough. We could see on Becca's face that she was struggling. Samuel didn't sleep well and he cried a lot and Becca always looked exhausted and on the edge of tears. I wished she would cry more, to let it out and show how she was feeling, but she seemed intent on holding it all in. I watched her bottom lip quiver and her eyes fill, watched her take a sharp breath in and shake her head, as if to dispel her own feelings. Was history repeating itself? Was she regretting motherhood, the way her mum had? I couldn't imagine her being a cold, distant mother, but I began to fear that she might become one.

And then one day, about six weeks in, Samuel smiled and it was different from the smiles he'd done before, that everyone said were down to wind, and Becca lit up from the inside, and I could see, for the first time, how much she loved him. The relief was strong. I felt like we'd handed Samuel over to her, for safekeeping, and I'd been hoping it hadn't been a mistake. Although, what was the alternative? For Samuel to never exist at all. There were no easy choices here.

One afternoon, Becca was checking her emails on her phone and there was one from school. Her dad was walking past and looked over her shoulder.

'Results?' he asked.

'I assume so.'

Ellie had messaged Becca a couple of days before, asking if she wanted to go to school together, to collect them. Becca had put her off. I knew what it was. She couldn't face going there with the buggy, with Samuel. Couldn't face everyone wanting to have a look at him and then talking about her behind her back.

'So...?' Her dad clearly wasn't going to let this drop.

Becca opened the email and looked at it for a long moment. 'A for History, and two Bs.'

Her dad let out a laugh, and I saw how nervous he'd been. 'Wow, Becca, that's brilliant!'

He hugged her, and she let him. She smiled and said she was pleased. But after he'd left, she sat down on the sofa and cried.

* * *

Ryan was around but somehow disengaged. He held Samuel but never asked Becca how she was doing. He didn't change a nappy unless he was asked to. Every day, I longed for him to step up, to become the man she clearly needed him to be. My future depended on it. One Saturday morning after a difficult night, they were lying in bed, all three of them, restless and exhausted.

'Can you take him through to the living room so I can get a bit more sleep?' Becca asked.

I could hear in her voice that it had cost her a lot to ask. She didn't usually, just dragged herself out of bed and got through the day as best she could.

'I'm tired too, you know,' Ryan said.

Becca closed her eyes briefly. Samuel was whimpering and it wouldn't be long before the whimper turned to a wail. She sat up, lifted Samuel into her arms and took him out of the room. We waited for Ryan to follow. He'd turned down her request of a lie-in, but surely he wouldn't take one for himself? But he did. There was no sign of him while Becca gave Samuel his first bottle, while she ate a cold piece of toast and butter, while she got out the playmat and laid him down on the floor and held things up to stimulate him. Her eyes were tired, but there was more than that. They were empty, too. I felt like she was going to break. Lucy and Thomas and I shared worried glances, but as usual, I felt like we were on either side of a wall. Them, campaigning for the end of this relationship. Me, hoping it might last a little longer. Just long enough.

Ryan wandered into the room an hour after Becca had got up. He was yawning, pulling a T-shirt over his head.

'Morning,' he said.

Becca didn't respond. I looked at her. She was furious. She was the one who'd been up in the night with Samuel. It had disturbed Ryan, of course, because they all slept in the same room, but it was her who had changed and fed and winded him. If she couldn't ask him for what she needed, if he couldn't give it to her, what was this union worth? I couldn't look at Lucy and Thomas. They hated him, Ryan, and they loved to be proved right, in moments like this. Sometimes it felt like they cared more about being right than they cared about Becca's happiness. As for me, I was still hoping that he would grow up, become better, learn what she needed and start giving it to her.

Ryan came further into the room. He kneeled down and

batted one of the soft toys that hung on an arch over Samuel's head. Samuel smiled, and Ryan stroked his cheek.

'What's up?' he asked, looking at Becca. 'Are you pissed off that I stayed in bed?'

'Yes, I'm pissed off,' she said. 'I'm shattered and fed up and pissed off.'

'You know I've been working all week?'

Becca stood up and it looked like she was going to leave the room. It wasn't a bad idea, I thought. Leave until you're calmer. But she'd never been one to back down from a confrontation.

'Ryan, I don't think you understand how this is for me. I'm at home with him all the time. I'm always feeding him or changing him or trying to entertain him, and I'm the one who does most of the night stuff, too. I need some support!'

'Babe, me working is support. If I didn't go to work, neither of you would have this flat to live in. You wouldn't have food to eat. I'm doing my share!'

Samuel started to cry a little and they both looked at him. Becca, from her standing position, Ryan from his place beside him on the floor. It was Becca who reached for him.

'It's okay, baby boy, Daddy's not cross with you. And neither am I. I'm sorry.' She held him against her chest and jiggled about, the way she'd learned he liked. This was a big part of being a mother, it seemed. Rocking, pushing, jiggling. Never still. Never at rest.

'I'm going to my dad's,' Becca said. 'Spend the whole day in bed if that's what you want.'

He didn't stop her. Not when she walked out of the room and not while she was packing a bag for Samuel. I wondered whether she'd thought he would. Whether she'd never really intended to go anywhere but had just wanted to push him into an apology. For my part, I was angry that he didn't even try to make her stay. He barely saw Samuel during the week with the hours he worked, and the weekend was their only time to be a family. Did he not want that? It was hard to face the fact that perhaps he didn't.

* * *

Becca and Samuel spent the day at her dad's house. He made them a nice lunch and they had a walk into town where he treated Becca to some posh chocolates and bought a new rattle for Samuel. He was besotted. It was a reminder of how he'd been when Becca was tiny; a welcome one. When he picked Samuel up and held him in his arms, looking down into his grandson's eyes, there was nothing there but pure, uncontaminated love. Purer, even, than Becca's.

'So why the visit?' her dad asked partway through the afternoon, when they were back at the house. 'What's Ryan up to?'

Becca must have known he would ask. She hadn't mentioned Ryan all day. But she didn't seem prepared for it. In fact, she looked like she would burst into tears. She was standing at the sink, washing Samuel's bottle so she could sterilise it in the microwave and make him a new one. And she just stopped, her hands plunged into the water.

'Is everything okay?' her dad asked, moving over to her and putting a hand on her shoulder.

'Not really. It's so hard, Dad. I didn't realise it would be so hard.'

Samuel was asleep in the pushchair, out in the hallway. When he was asleep, it always seemed ludicrous that things were so difficult, but when he was awake, we saw it.

'I know,' her dad said. 'Come here.'

Becca took her soapy hands from the bowl and turned, and

her dad put his arms around her and she held onto him, the bubbles dripping down his back.

'I feel so stupid. Everyone tried to tell me, but I thought I knew better.'

'And is Ryan— Does he understand that you're struggling?'

Something in Becca's face changed a little at that. 'I didn't say I was struggling. That makes it sound like I can't do it, like I don't want to do it.'

Her dad held his hands up in surrender. They were standing a few inches apart. 'I didn't mean that. I just meant, does he know how you feel?'

Becca shrugged. 'I asked him to let me sleep a bit this morning and somehow *he* ended up having a lie-in.'

This was a betrayal and it was clear that Becca felt a bit uncomfortable sharing it. It was possible that in a few months' time, everything between her and Ryan would seem okay, and she would wish her dad didn't have this thing she'd told him to hold against her boyfriend. But at the same time, she was an eighteen-year-old girl who was finding it hard to be a mum and she needed someone who was unreservedly on her side. And that person was her dad. It always would be.

'What can I do?' he asked. 'Do you want me to have a word with him?'

'No, that won't help.'

'Well, what then, Bec? I need to know you're going to be okay. I worry about you so much, the two of you.'

'Me and Ryan?'

'You and Samuel.'

Lines were drawn. Becca had always known that her dad wasn't keen on the situation, but this was the closest he'd come to saying that he wasn't keen on Ryan.

'I will be okay. We will be. I just... I just wish he would help a bit more.'

'Then tell him, darling. Be honest with him, like you've been with me. If he's any sort of a man, he'll step up and support you. And if he doesn't, well, you know where to find me. I'll always be here.'

'What do you mean by that?' Becca didn't look angry, just confused.

'I mean that if he lets you down, or you decide he's not the right one for you, I will do whatever I can to support you and that little man out there. I love you more than I can say, and I love him too, and I will be here for you no matter what happens.'

Becca put her hands to her face for a moment. 'It's all about getting rid of him, isn't it? You want him out of my life, and the moment I say that things aren't absolutely perfect, you seize on it and use it as a way to push your own agenda.'

Her dad sighed. 'Becca, that's not what I'm doing. I accept that you and Ryan are together. You're a family, the three of you. I'm just saying that he needs to do his bit and I will be here if you need me, that's all.'

They stood opposite one another, both leaning back against the kitchen's worktops. Stalemate.

'I think it's probably time we got home,' Becca said.

'Because it's actually time you got home or because of what I just said?'

'A bit of both. But thank you for today, Dad.' Becca started to gather their things.

'I thought he was due a feed soon.'

'I'll do it at home. It won't take us long to get there, and he's still asleep.'

Her dad looked tired and ready to give up. Not on Becca,

not on Samuel, but on this disagreement. He helped Becca to pack up and saw her to the door.

'You can come here anytime, you know that,' he said as she pushed the buggy out of the door.

'I know,' she said. 'Bye, Dad.'

* * *

The following week, out of the blue, Becca's mum turned up at the flat.

'I'm sorry,' she said, standing on the doorstep. 'I'm sorry I haven't been around much.'

Becca invited her in and asked her to hold Samuel while she made them some tea. I watched Liz, watched the way she held her grandson, as if she wasn't quite sure how. If I hadn't known her for eighteen years, if she wasn't the mother of the woman who might be my mother, I would say she'd never had a baby, never been a mother herself.

When they were sitting on the sofa and Becca was feeding Samuel, her mum crossed her legs and started to speak, and it was as if she'd rehearsed it, as if she'd come to say this thing and she was determined to get it out.

'I'm not very good at this, Becca, at any of it. I'm sorry for what I said, when your dad and I told you we were splitting up. I'm sorry if it hurt you, but now that you're a mother I wonder whether perhaps you'll see it from my perspective a little more easily. I wasn't a natural mum. I didn't enjoy it, didn't get a feel for it as I went along. I felt like I was floundering, all through your childhood.'

Becca had said to her dad, on occasion, that she wanted to talk to her mum, to hear what she had to say, but I wondered whether she really wanted this. Surely it was too much, too much honesty, too close to the bone.

'It's hard,' Becca said. 'It's so much harder than I thought it would be. I had no idea. But I love him...' She left a pause, and I thought it was probably a bit of space for her mum to say that she had loved Becca, but she didn't. 'I love him and I just know I have to do what's right for him, so I get on with it.'

They both looked at Samuel. He'd finished his bottle and he was drifting off to sleep in Becca's arms. Every now and again, his eyes would open and then they'd roll back in his head.

'I just never found my feet,' her mum said. 'It wasn't for lack of trying.'

'Where were you on the morning he was born?' Becca asked.

Her mum shifted a little in her seat. She put a hand to her mouth and touched her lips, and then placed her hands back in her lap. 'I was at home,' she admitted. 'I was sitting at the table in my kitchen, trying to gear myself up to come. All my life, I feel like I've been trying to gear myself up to be the mother you need.'

'All I needed was for you to be there,' Becca said.

'I know.'

It was clear, then, that the visit wasn't going to last much longer, and that it wasn't the start of a new pattern, one in which Becca's mum would come round more often and take Samuel to the park or go with Becca to choose his first pair of shoes. It was an admission, a clearing of the air. But it wasn't a promise of anything else.

When she got up to leave, Becca's mum looked down at her daughter and her grandson. 'Don't get up,' she said. 'He looks so peaceful. I can show myself out.'

I looked hard at Becca and I could see that she was waiting for some kind of approval. For her mum to say that she was doing a good job, that Becca was the natural mum she had never managed to be, but she didn't say anything, and Becca would never have asked for it. For a long time after she heard the click of the door closing, Becca sat very still, a confused sadness on her face. And when Samuel woke with a stretch and a cry, she stood up and got on with her day.

10

DECEMBER 2022

Lucy came to me on a drizzly Saturday morning in December when Becca and Samuel were at the park. Christmas was close, but the weather wasn't delivering those crisp, frosty days yet. Just damp and rain. Lucy and I were hovering near the swings, where Becca was pushing Samuel. He had a huge grin on his face. Thomas wasn't with us. I wasn't sure why we'd come, to be honest. Becca and Ryan had had a huge fight because he didn't want to go out and Samuel so obviously needed a bit of fresh air. In the end, Becca had stomped about, gathering things together, and then pushed Samuel out of the door in the buggy without saying goodbye. Lucy and I had exchanged a weary look and followed. Just because there was nothing else to do. When Lucy started to speak, I thought it was going to be about that. I thought she was going to tell me, again, how bad Ryan was for Becca and how she wished they'd split up. I couldn't have imagined what she actually had to say.

'Eliza, there's something I've been meaning to tell you,' she started.

It sounded serious. But more than that, it sounded ominous.

'I told Thomas and he said I had to tell you.'

I wondered, vaguely, when this conversation had happened, but there was no way of knowing. Samuel and I had had secret chats all the time when he was still here with us. The hours were long and yawning, for us. We couldn't read a book or watch TV or take up a hobby. We didn't have jobs or go to school. We had all these hours to think and watch and wait. And talk.

'What is it?' I asked.

'I lied to you. When we first arrived, when Becca was born, I mean. I lied to all of you, about my conception date.'

I hadn't been expecting that. How could I have been? What would have possessed her to tell us the wrong date? We didn't know anything back then, hadn't encountered Ryan or Anthony. How could she have known that there was any point in keeping her conception date a secret?

'Why?'

I was genuinely baffled. I couldn't think of a single reason why she would have done that. The date she'd told us was a couple of years after mine, and the four of us had talked over and over about the chances of each of us being born. Samuel first, with Ryan as his father, then Thomas, with Anthony as his. Me, with Ryan again, then Lucy, with Anthony. We'd all known that it was unlikely that Becca would go back and forth like that. So what was Lucy about to say? How was she about to change this fact that I'd always known?

'I panicked,' Lucy said. 'You said your date, and it was so close to mine, I just blurted out something else. I didn't think it through. And then once I'd said it, I couldn't really go back.'

So close to mine. How close?

'What is your date?' I asked, my voice a little mechanical. I had to know, then. I had to know what we were dealing with.

'It's the fifth of January,' she said.

Fifth of January.

'What year?'

'2025.'

I understood, then. Her conception date was just a few months after mine. There was no way that both of us could be born. And she'd known this for our entire lives, and waited until now to let me in on the secret.

'Did Samuel know?' I asked.

It was a strange question. But I couldn't bear to think of them all discussing this, me the only one on the outside. I couldn't bear to think that he might have kept something like this from me.

'No, of course not. I only told Thomas the other day. It's been gnawing at me for years, but I just didn't know how to fix it.'

'What did Thomas say?' Would Thomas have been on my side in this? I always thought of him and Lucy as a pair.

'It was a way of testing the water, telling him,' she went on, as if she hadn't even heard me. 'It doesn't affect him, really.'

How could she say it didn't affect him? It meant that only one of us could ever be his sister.

'And he said I needed to talk to you about it. He told me to tell you.'

I wanted to ask whether she'd have ever got around to telling me if he hadn't pushed her to. But what was the point? Of course she would say that she would have done. There was nothing to be gained.

'So...' I said.

'I'm so sorry, Eliza. If I could go back and tell the truth from the start, I would. I had no idea. We were just starting out and we didn't know each other yet, and I guess I thought it would set us up as enemies if we always knew that only one of us could be born.'

'But you knew...' I said.

'Yes. I knew.'

It felt as if she'd had the upper hand for all these years. Perhaps she had. I thought again about the timeline. Much more feasible for Becca and Ryan to split up and her to have two children with Anthony than for her to keep going back and forth. And they were on the verge of splitting, as far as we could tell. My thoughts must have been clear to read on my face, because Lucy looked sympathetically at me.

'I'm sorry,' she said.

'That you didn't tell me or that you're so sure you're the one who's going to be born?' I asked.

She had every reason to be confident, it was true, but you just never knew what was going to happen. She looked surprised by my little outburst.

'I'm not sure of anything,' she said.

But I think we both knew she was.

* * *

Becca was putting Samuel back in the buggy to take him home. We followed, glumly. What would we find when we got there? Would Ryan be there? Would they continue the argument they'd had that morning or find a way to make up? I felt like I was seeing everything differently now I knew Lucy's secret. I felt like I was looking at it all through a lens, and everything had come into sharp focus. Lucy must be loving this, all these rows and this uncertainty about the future of their relationship.

On the walk home, I looked out for Christmas lights. Looped around trees and bushes, hung up on the fronts of houses. They were turned off, and they dripped with rainwater. Christmas cheer felt a long way away.

Becca opened the door to the flat and stepped inside. She left the buggy in the hallway, where they kept it, although there was barely space for it, and she lifted Samuel out and carried him through to the living area. Ryan was playing on his Xbox, his feet up on the coffee table. Becca looked at him from the doorway for a minute. Was she waiting for him to pause his game and look at her, to ask her where she'd been, to apologise? He did none of those things. She set Samuel down on the floor and put a few cushions around him. He was learning to sit up then, and he'd sometimes topple over with no warning.

'Hey, little man,' Ryan said.

And still he carried on playing. It was a zombie game, and he'd been playing it for weeks, trying to get a bit further each night after Becca went to bed.

'I need to talk to you,' Becca said.

Ryan didn't look at her. 'Give me a second,' he said.

She didn't respond. Just stood there, waiting, her arms folded.

Finally, he paused the game and turned to face her. 'Is this about earlier?' he asked. 'I just didn't fancy going out, that's all. I've had a long week...'

'I've had a long week too,' she said. 'Do you think I fancied a trip to the park? Do you think it was what I really wanted to do on a drizzly Saturday morning? I went because it's all about Sammy, now. He needed to get out. He can't be stuck in this flat all day long.'

'Listen, Becca, I feel like we had this argument before you went out and I don't really want to have it again.'

He stood up. Becca was standing in the doorway and he pushed his way past her, went into the bedroom. Becca followed him. I felt scared, all of a sudden. He had his faults, Ryan, he had more than his fair share of faults, but he'd never hurt her, never done anything physical. But then, for a second, I thought perhaps he could. I looked on, fear creeping in me.

'This isn't working,' Becca said.

Ryan was rooting through his pile of clothes on the floor. He often did this. He'd leave a tenner in his jeans pocket and then forget where he'd put it. But he stopped when she said that, and stood up.

'What isn't working?'

'This. All of this. I feel like I'm a single mum. I didn't go into this expecting to do it all on my own.'

Ryan sat down on the edge of the bed. 'You're not doing it on your own. Who do you think is paying for us to live here?'

Becca rolled her eyes. 'It's not enough, Ryan. I know you work hard but you have a family, too. You can't just come home and expect to have all your time off to yourself, because that's not how it works.'

Samuel wailed, then, and they both went into the living room. He'd fallen back onto the cushions. He wasn't hurt, but it always startled him to end up horizontal, especially if there was no one with him to sit him back up. Becca reached him and picked him up. Despite the fall, he still had a plastic phone in one hand. She took it from him, held it to her ear.

'For me?' she asked. 'Hello? Yes, it's Sammy's mummy. Okay, I'll tell him.'

She crouched down. 'Granddad says he loves you.'

Samuel beamed and took the phone and Becca sat him back down again, checked the cushions were all in place.

'You don't play with him,' Becca said, turning to Ryan and starting to cry. 'You never play with him.'

'You're just better at that stuff than me,' Ryan said.

'No, I'm not. It's just that I do it. That's the only difference. I'm eighteen and I didn't know how to be a mum, and I had to learn because I became one. And you haven't bothered to learn how to be a dad. We're going to move out.'

Ryan stood up. He moved across the room and took her in his arms and she cried into his chest.

'Where will you go?' he asked.

Becca looked up, and I could see in her eyes that she was surprised. She'd expected him to at least fight for her. For them.

'Back to my dad's.'

'I didn't think it would be like this,' Ryan said. 'The baby thing. It's really, really hard.'

Lucy's rage was almost a living thing. I could feel it, beside me. 'It's not hard for him! He doesn't even do it!' she cried out.

And she was right, but it wasn't the time. I was watching my parents break up, and I was two years away from conception, and it was looking very likely that I would never be born at all.

'I'll call my dad,' Becca said. 'Make sure it's okay.'

She went into the living room, scooped up Samuel, and returned to the bedroom to make the phone call. She was still crying, but quietly now.

'Dad?' we heard her say a little shakily. 'It's over, with Ryan. Can Sammy and I come to stay with you for a bit?'

And just like that, it was done.

11

MARCH 2023

There were a handful of weeks to go before Thomas's conception date, and Becca and Samuel were settling back into her dad's house. Thomas was worried, but he tried not to let it show. There had been no sign of Anthony, Thomas's father, for a long time.

'But at least she's single,' Lucy kept saying when she tried to reassure him. 'If she was still with Ryan, it would be worse.'

I knew what she meant, but it hurt to hear her talk about my parents' relationship like that. I looked at Samuel sometimes and wondered whether he had any sense of it. Of the fact that his parents had parted before he was even old enough to walk. It was sad, wasn't it? Becca thought it was sad, that much was clear. She'd been moping around. Staying in her pyjamas when she wasn't going anywhere, dressing in jeans and oversized cardigans when she had to go out. She hadn't worn makeup for weeks.

'It isn't going to happen,' Thomas said one day when we were watching Becca spoon some kind of vegetable mush into Samuel's mouth.

It was the first time he'd said it out loud. We all must have thought it, at one time or another. Lucy and I turned his way.

'I mean, look at her. Does she look like she's about to fall headlong into a new relationship? Or have a one-night stand with someone she knew at school, even? She never goes anywhere, other than to the occasional baby group. It's impossible.'

Inside, I agreed with every word he said. But I didn't want to dash any hope he might have left. 'Don't forget you have your Chance,' I said.

'But how? With who?' He'd obviously given it a lot of thought. Of course he had. This was his battle to live.

I looked at Lucy. She often thought of things we didn't. It was like she looked at the world from a slightly different angle, and it sometimes helped when it came to thinking up good ideas.

'What about Anthony?' she asked.

'What about him?' Thomas asked, his expression confused.

'What if you focus on him, rather than her? I mean, we always talk about inhabiting the body of her dad or her friend or whatever, but what if you inhabit his? Can you change the way someone thinks, from inside? Put the idea of her in his head? Make him resolve to find her?'

It was certainly a new idea. I had no clue whether it could work. It was risky. But Thomas looked like he was considering it carefully.

'What if I do it, and it doesn't work?' Thomas asked.

Lucy didn't say anything. Thomas looked from her to me. There was nothing we could say that he didn't already know. But he looked like he needed to hear it anyway.

'That's the risk we all take, isn't it? You just have to give it a try.'

'What about that thing you can do, Eliza?' Thomas asked suddenly.

'What thing?'

'Where you make Becca do something. Can you still do that?'

'I think so,' I said. 'I haven't tried it for a while. But it was only little things, you know. I'm not sure I can make her find Anthony and sleep with him.'

I was going for humour, but nobody laughed.

'Will you help me, if I think of a way?'

He looked at me, and I thought about saying no. It wasn't that I wanted to. I was just curious, about what would happen. What he would say. What effect it would have on him and Lucy, and me. On the fragile dynamic between the three of us, which seemed ever more precarious since Lucy had let me in on her secret. And then I said the only thing I possibly could.

'Of course I'll help you.'

* * *

The next day, Becca went into town. This wasn't unusual. We had no reason to expect that anything out of the ordinary was about to happen. She didn't have much money, but she liked having a mooch around, pushing the buggy in and out of shops, daydreaming (I always suspected) about what she would buy if she had the money. Her dad had slipped her a twenty-pound note a few days previously and told her to buy something for Samuel or for herself. He'd raised his eyebrows when he'd said that last bit. He was trusting her to spend the money where it was needed. And I'd known, that day, that a trip to town would be on the cards.

She spent ages in the kids' section of H&M, choosing

between a pair of skinny jeans with a stripy blue and white top and a little grey jacket covered in red stars. She held them up for Samuel to see, asked what he thought. I'd hoped she would spend the money on herself, had thought she might. Over the years, almost all her money had gone on clothes and makeup. Shopping trips with Ellie. But since Samuel, she'd had less money than ever, and it had all gone on him. She chose the outfit in the end, went to the till and paid. The cashier took her twenty-pound note and handed back a fiver and some coins as change.

Becca headed back onto the high street. I thought she was going to go straight home but she ducked into a café and ordered a pot of tea and a shortbread biscuit in the shape of a star. She pulled a bag of rice cakes from the changing bag and handed one to Samuel whenever he started to grizzle. This was a little luxury she wasn't used to, and I was glad. She looked happier, I thought. Content. Still so young to be a mum, but settling into it. Finding her way.

When the door opened and she looked up and Anthony walked in, we were all equally shocked. Me, Lucy, Thomas and Becca. I turned to Thomas.

'Did you have anything to do with this?' I asked.

'No,' he said urgently. It was clear he didn't want to miss anything. Neither did I.

Becca hadn't seen Anthony since she was pregnant, since New Year's Eve. What did he think, this boy who had once seemed so interested in her? I could feel the tension coming off Thomas in waves. I didn't look at him again. Couldn't. This had the potential to set things on an entirely different course.

He didn't see her at first. He went to the counter as she had, ordered a coffee and a sandwich. And it was only when he was looking around for a spare table that he spotted her. They both froze for a moment, and then his face broke into an easy smile and he headed over to her table.

'Can I sit with you?' he asked.

A couple of years earlier, he might have asked this in the school canteen. Now, there was a buggy beside the table. Anthony peered into it.

'What's his name?' Anthony asked, at the same time that Becca said, 'Yes.'

They smiled at each other, and there was something in it beyond an acknowledgement of their talking over one another. There was something shared. To me, it looked like they were both remembering that they could have had something. Could have been something. I willed Becca to remember that if she'd got together with Anthony, she wouldn't have had Samuel, although that was more complicated than repeating a simple instruction over and over, and I had no hope that it would work.

Anthony sat down. He stirred two sachets of sugar into his coffee and asked Becca how she was. And then he looked up at her because she hadn't answered. I looked at her, too. I thought she was going to cry.

'I'm okay,' Becca said. 'Ryan and I broke up. I'm back at home.'

She looked, immediately after, like she realised that she'd said too much. He'd only asked how she was, and she could have stopped after saying she was okay. He hadn't asked for the ins and outs.

'Sorry to hear that,' Anthony said.

He didn't look particularly sorry. I wondered whether he still liked her. It seemed like he might. And if he thought she'd said too much, he didn't show it. Becca looked like she didn't know what to say next, and he rescued her by speaking again.

'What's it like then? Being a mum?'

What was it like? How would she choose to frame it? Would she talk about the endless nappy changing, the broken sleep, the drudgery? Or the way Samuel looked at her like she was the whole world? The pure joy of watching him learn a new skill, breath held?

'It's mostly good,' she said without much conviction. 'What are you doing now? How's uni?'

'I love it,' he said. 'Just home for Easter.'

He leaned back in his chair and took a long gulp of his coffee. I watched Becca. She was still drawn to him, I thought. There was still something there. He wasn't traditionally handsome in the way that Ryan was. He was taller, verging on gangly, and he had a long nose and longish, unkempt hair. But when he smiled, he lit up. And I saw Becca seeing that, responding to it. Lighting up a little herself, at the proximity of him.

What was there to say? Their lives had taken them in two directions that couldn't have been more different, and what common ground there might have been with shared memories of school had been more or less eroded. Anthony was meeting new people and learning new things, and at the end of it he would probably get a good job. And where would Becca be, then? Still a mum. Still living with her dad? We didn't know.

They might never meet again. Perhaps it would have been better, I thought, if they hadn't met that day. Of course, this wasn't how Thomas and Lucy wanted it to go. They would be seeing this chance meeting as a turning point, as the beginning of something better. They would be pleading, silently, for them to ask each other whether they still had the same phone numbers and to admit, somehow, that there was still something between them.

'Do you still listen to the Beatles?' Anthony asked.

And Becca looked taken by surprise. Happily so. 'I haven't for a long time,' she said.

'I was listening to *Sgt. Pepper* the other day, and I thought of you. "She's Leaving Home". You're right. It's a brilliant song. Did you know it was based on a newspaper story?'

Becca nodded. 'Yes.' If she was pleased about this reminder of the way they had shared Beatles facts in the past, she didn't show it.

'Would you have gone to uni, do you think, if you hadn't had the baby?' Anthony asked.

Samuel chose that moment to start whining, and the bag of rice cakes was empty. Becca unstrapped him and took him into her arms. He wriggled and moaned, and eventually she gave up and put him down on the floor, where he crawled from one table to the next. Becca kept her eyes on him, ready to swoop in and pick him up, set him back on track. This was her job, and I could see how it exhausted her. It wasn't only all the things she did, and those were many, but the things she had to be ready to do, if needed. It was the constant need to be alert that almost killed you, it seemed.

'I don't know,' she said. 'I can't imagine it, now. I was going to take a year out and then decide.'

'What would you have studied, if you did go?'

Becca paused, and I wasn't sure whether she was considering the question or something else. 'I don't know, Anthony,' she said eventually.

It was sharp, the way she said it, and sad. Anthony looked taken aback.

'I'm sorry,' he said, 'I didn't mean...'

'No, I'm sorry. It's just, what's the point in talking about a life I can't have? Talking about what I would have done if I hadn't been so stupid as to get knocked up? I know that's what you think, what everyone thinks. And it's done now, so it's too late. It just doesn't help anyone to pretend and imagine what could have been.'

It was the most she'd said since the exchange had begun, and both of them seemed surprised by it. Anthony reached a hand across the table and put it, flat, on top of hers, and she looked at him for a second.

'I don't think that,' he said. 'And I didn't mean to upset you. I was just curious. I was thinking you could go back, later, and do it then. There isn't one right way, one order to live your life in. When you're in your mid-thirties, Samuel will be grown up, and other people will just be starting out with all that. Who's to say what you might do then?'

There was a wail, and they both looked over to where Samuel was sitting on the floor. Becca jumped up and retrieved him, but not before the woman sitting at a nearby table had shaken her head and tutted, as if to say that Becca was not a good mother because she had allowed her baby son to tip over on his padded, nappy-clad bottom.

I wanted to hug Becca. I wanted to tell her that she was doing great, that she was almost a miracle to me, to us. I wanted her to know that she was more than an eighteen-year-old with few qualifications who'd messed up her future by having a baby so young. I wanted her to know that being a mother was a wonderful thing.

'I have to go,' Becca said. She kissed Samuel's forehead and slotted him back into the buggy, but he writhed about when she tried to do the straps up, and I could see her face getting redder.

'Stay,' Anthony said. 'Or come for a walk with me. Will he be happier outside?'

'He will, but we need to get home anyway. I've got stuff to do.'

Anthony stood up to say goodbye and Becca let him hug her, but it was just his arms around her, her own arms hanging limply at her sides. Samuel was screaming now, full of rage at being imprisoned.

'Look after yourself, Becca Valentine,' Anthony said.

But who could look after themselves when there was a small child to be looked after? It didn't seem to work, as far as I could see.

On the walk home, Becca let the tears fall and I was glad. They had to go somewhere, tears, and if they didn't come out when they needed to, I thought they only made things worse in the long run.

12

MARCH 2023

Thomas was different after that day. Even though Becca and Anthony hadn't made plans to see each other again, he had a quiet confidence. That meeting had taken us all by surprise, and now who knew what would happen next? The way Samuel had been conceived, when it had looked so unlikely, had given us all hope. So I'm not sure any of us were shocked when Becca was scrolling through Instagram one evening and a notification appeared to tell her she had a new follower, and it was Anthony. She looked at his profile picture for a few seconds before responding. In it, he was standing alone at the top of some hill or mountain, his arms raised in a cheer. He looked relaxed, happy. She hovered over the follow back button, then clicked it.

He sent her a message about half an hour later. Lucy joked that he'd had it ready but hadn't wanted to look too keen. I felt left out of something. They saw this as their happy ever after, and it certainly wasn't mine. But that didn't stop me from reading the message over her shoulder, just as they did.

Hey Becca, it was nice to see you the other day. I'm sorry if
I upset you, asking about your plans for the future. Could I
take you out for a drink sometime to apologise? Or if it's
hard to get a babysitter, a daytime trip to the park? Anthony.

It was a nice message, a thoughtful one. He'd acknowledged
that it might be hard for her to go out with him because of
Samuel. He was showing her that he understood that it didn't
bother him, that he was willing to work around it. How many
twenty-year-olds would be? We were surprised when Becca put
her phone down without replying, but none of us missed the
smile on her face. It was the closest she'd looked to happy since
she'd split up with Ryan. Longer, probably. Looking back, I
realised I hadn't seen her looking uncomplicatedly happy for a
long time. Samuel was always making her smile, but there was
often a sadness behind it, because he was a reminder of Ryan,
and that was a reminder that things hadn't worked out. That
she'd left, just like her mother had.

I knew she'd respond to the message. She just didn't want to
appear too eager, I thought. And sure enough, once a couple of
hours had passed and she'd put Samuel down for the night, she
picked up her phone again and wrote him a message.

Hi Anthony, it was good to see you too. And I'm sorry I got
all defensive. I know you didn't mean anything by it. It would
be really nice to get out one evening – I feel like I'm climbing
the walls sometimes. I'll ask Dad if he can look after Sammy
for me. Talk soon, Becca.

It was set in motion. It was happening. And after that, there
was a lot of messaging and it all seemed so inevitable, somehow. They chose a date; settled on going to the cinema. I

realised, when they were making the arrangements, that although Becca had a child, she'd barely been on any proper dates. With Ryan, they had moved so fast from meeting at a party to being a proper couple and living together. There had been that dinner in a restaurant on her eighteenth birthday. They had never once held hands in a cinema. I wondered whether Becca had thought of that.

When the day arrived, she got progressively nervous as the hours passed. She made a series of small, silly mistakes, like giving Samuel his dinner without warming it first, and forgetting the one thing she'd gone to the supermarket for. And when her dad finally intervened, lifting Samuel out of her arms and telling her to go and get ready before she did 'some serious damage', Becca looked relieved. She went upstairs to her bedroom, sat down on the edge of her bed, took a deep breath.

'This is important to her,' Lucy said.

I'd just been thinking the same thing, but I didn't like hearing it spoken aloud.

'How long until your date again?' I asked Thomas.

It was so hard to keep all the dates in my mind.

'Three weeks,' he said. 'I mean, they need to get a move on, but it's looking pretty good, don't you think?'

He was asking for reassurance but I couldn't give it. I didn't say anything, and when the silence got too awkward, Lucy stepped in.

'Really good,' she said. 'I'm sure you've got nothing to worry about.'

I felt like that was overstating it a bit. They were going on a date, yes, and they both seemed keen, but I wouldn't have wanted to bet on the fact that they'd be sleeping together in three weeks' time. I stayed quiet, because I knew that anything

I had to say would be hurtful to Thomas. Would seem like bitterness.

It was unusual for Becca to be alone in a room for any length of time. That was what it was like for mums, I'd come to learn. So her dad had really given her a gift, that afternoon, by taking Samuel off her hands early. She had a bath, a long, lazy one, and then she spent a good ten minutes looking in her wardrobe and trying to decide what to wear. This was the old Becca. The carefree one. It seemed ironic, in a way, that a date with someone from school was bringing it out in her.

She settled on skinny jeans and a simple black top, then added some colour with ballet pumps and earrings, both in bright, postbox red. I was so used to seeing her in her slouchy mum clothes that I was taken aback. She was still a little heavier than she'd been before the pregnancy, but she'd settled into it, and it suited her. She was standing taller, dressed like that, looking confident. It was a transformation. By the time she'd done her makeup, she looked almost like someone else. It was unsettling.

'She looks amazing,' Lucy said. 'I can't remember the last time she looked that good.'

We were all staring. Gone were the leggings and baggy jumpers she'd been living in, not just since she'd moved home, but since she'd become a mum. And under them, this beauty had been lurking, unseen.

Anthony had said he'd pick her up at seven, and the doorbell went at five minutes to. Becca swore under her breath. It wasn't that she wasn't ready. She'd finished off by pinning back some of her hair, and had looked at herself hard in the mirror. Why was she so nervous? I could only imagine it was because this night meant a lot to her. And that thought made me feel a bit wobbly, a bit knocked off-balance. I felt almost like I was slowly fading away.

When she went downstairs, Anthony was standing in the hallway talking to her dad. Samuel was in her dad's arms and Anthony kept looking at him and reaching a finger out to touch his nose. Samuel was delighted.

'Hi,' Becca said, walking down the stairs.

Anthony looked up at her and smiled widely. He was wearing jeans and a faded T-shirt under a jacket, and Becca looked relieved to see that she hadn't over or underdressed.

'Ready to go?' he asked. 'You look lovely.'

Becca glanced at her dad, who smiled and made a sort of shooing motion to show that Becca should go. Then Becca leaned in and kissed the top of Samuel's head.

'Be good, little man.'

Anthony turned and Becca followed him out of the door and to his car, an old Volkswagen Beetle, and they got in, both silent.

'Are you okay?' Anthony asked, looking behind him to pull away.

They'd been so chatty on Instagram. But it was probably easier, I thought, when you didn't have to look at the person.

'Sorry, I'm fine. I'm just not used to this. I can't remember the last time I went out without Sammy. And I certainly haven't worn eyeliner since before he was born.'

Anthony laughed. 'Look, it's just a film. Nothing big or dramatic.'

'Thank you,' Becca said, and Anthony took his eyes off the road for a moment to look at her, perplexed.

'For what?'

'For understanding.'

* * *

They held hands in the cinema, shared popcorn. Thomas was delighted. Lucy too. Could this be it, the ending they'd wished for, so soon? When the film ended, neither Becca nor Anthony moved. They sat in the dark, holding hands, while the credits rolled up the screen and the people around them got up and left. They moved their feet to one side so the people in their aisle could squeeze past them. Only when the cinema was empty did Anthony speak.

'Do you want to go for a drive?' he asked.

Becca turned her face to him. 'You know I have a baby, right?'

Anthony nodded slowly. 'Er, yes, I know you have a baby.'

'So you know it's not that simple, being with me.'

'Who said I was looking for simple?'

Becca pulled her hand away from Anthony's, sat up a little straighter.

'You're going back to uni soon,' she said. 'I feel like you just want this thing, with me, because you couldn't have me back then, when I met Ryan. I feel like maybe it's just something you want to tick off, before you go away and forget about this town and me and everything else.'

Just then, the lights sputtered into life. Becca blinked several times, adjusting.

'That's a lot of assumptions you've made there,' Anthony said. He reached for her hand but then thought better of it and left it lying where it was, next to her thigh. 'Look, Becca. I like you. I've always liked you. I don't care about scoring points or ticking things off. I'm just here, out with a girl I really like, and I don't want the evening to be over yet, so I'm asking her to come for a drive with me. That's all.'

'So you're not expecting me to sleep with you?' Becca asked. There was a smile in her voice, but it hadn't reached her face yet.

'I'm not expecting anything.'

I glanced at Thomas, but his expression was hard to read.

'Okay then,' she said. 'Let's drive.'

They left the cinema, Becca first and Anthony following, and walked back to Anthony's car. They didn't speak. When they got inside and he plugged his phone in, the car was flooded with the sound of 'Love Me Do'. He reached to turn the volume down to a reasonable level, and they both laughed. It broke the tension a little.

'Did you know Paul McCartney was sixteen when they wrote this song?' Becca asked.

'Yes. Did you know it's the first song they recorded?'

'Yes,' Becca said, laughing.

I thought maybe she was lying, but if Anthony thought so too, he didn't pick her up on it.

'How did you get into them?'

'My dad,' Becca said. 'He used to sing their songs to me when I was a baby and wouldn't sleep. I feel like they kind of seeped in.'

Anthony smiled, and I saw something in his expression that I'd never seen before. He had a quiet confidence, just like I'd noticed in Thomas. He was willing to wait. And I was as sure as he seemed, in that moment, that he would get his girl.

'Where are we going?' he asked.

Becca shrugged. 'Wherever you like.'

So Anthony turned out of the car park and started driving out of town, in the direction of London, and they began to talk. Simple stuff that they'd never covered. Their childhoods, their families. Holidays, pets, siblings, or lack of them. And then, as the miles clocked up, the less concrete things. Beliefs, hurts, fears. Love.

'Do you want to have children one day?' Becca asked.

'Of course. A boy called Lennon...'

Becca laughed.

'Maybe not. But I definitely want to have kids. What about you? Do you want more?'

'I think so.'

'Got any names picked out?'

'I like Lucy. And not just because of the Beatles song.'

Anthony nodded. 'Lucy,' he said, as if mulling it over.

I looked at Lucy, couldn't help it. She looked like she couldn't quite take it in, like it was too much all at once. And I felt spiteful, all of a sudden, and wanted to ruin it.

'It's like a backwards step,' I said. 'From living with her boyfriend to going out for a drive with a guy. It feels like she's going back in time, back to being a teenager.'

I said it a little sneeringly, but that wasn't the way Lucy interpreted it.

'Yes,' Lucy said, 'it does, doesn't it? Isn't that wonderful?'

* * *

'I need to start heading back,' Becca said.

It was after eleven, and they were miles from home. Anthony turned left without saying anything.

'I'm sorry, it's not that I'm not having a good time, it's just...'

'I know,' Anthony said. 'Samuel. I understand.'

'Can we do it again?' she asked, after a minute of silence.

Had she had to work up to that? Had she had to make herself say it?

'We can do it again whenever you like,' Anthony replied.

'Like you said, I'm going back to Bristol soon, but I can come home at weekends and we get a lot of holidays.'

'There's no one there you could go out with?' Becca asked. 'Wouldn't that be simpler?'

Anthony sighed and then smiled to show her he wasn't annoyed. 'I'm sure it probably would be, yes. But I like you, and you're here.'

And Becca smiled, and her face was alight, and I realised again that I hadn't seen her smile like that for a really long time. Just an honest, genuine smile. Uncomplicated happiness.

On the drive back, Becca fell asleep. When Anthony pulled up outside her house, he touched her shoulder gently, and she opened her eyes.

'Shit, was I asleep?'

'Fast asleep. Snoring. The works.'

Becca pushed his shoulder with a smile on her face and it felt like the kind of thing she wouldn't do with Ryan.

'Thank you,' she said. 'I've had a really nice time.'

'Me too.'

'Can I ask you something?'

'Of course.'

'What did you have planned, that night that we were supposed to meet up?'

Anthony put his head in his hands. 'Oh god, I'm embarrassed to tell you. I had this sort of treasure hunt set up, all over the town. And we were going to end up at that Italian restaurant, the one that used to be near the library, and I'd asked Ellie what you liked and had pre-ordered everything and they were going to bring it out when we arrived.'

Becca looked shocked. 'I can't believe you went to all that trouble.'

Anthony gave her a direct look. 'It wasn't any trouble. I'm just sorry we never got to have the date.'

'You've said that enough. You know, that was the night my parents told me they were splitting up, and I was so upset. And then you didn't come, and I'd pinned all my teenage hope on you, I think. I went to a party and got drunk and that's where I met Ryan and... well, you know the rest.'

Neither of them said anything while Becca unclipped her seatbelt and reached for the door handle.

'I thought you might try to kiss me,' Becca said, at last.

'Do you want me to try to kiss you?'

'Do you want to try to kiss me?'

Anthony laughed. 'God, yes.'

He leaned across the space between them and I saw how his seatbelt was cutting into his neck. He kissed Becca gently on the lips, and then, when they parted, he kissed her more deeply. A little urgently. They'd both waited for this for a long time. And they made the most of it, their arms snaking around one another's bodies. At some point, Becca unclipped Anthony's seatbelt so he was more free to move.

'I want to do things with you,' Becca said, her face flushed.

'I want to do things with you, too,' Anthony laughed.

'But not tonight. I'll call you.' She leaned in, kissed him one last time, and then she opened the door and got out of the car.

'Goodnight, Becca Valentine,' he called, and she gave him a little wave before turning away and getting her key out of her bag.

13

APRIL 2023

'What if she's scared to rush into anything, to rush into having sex with someone new, I mean, because she got pregnant the very first time she did?' Thomas asked. 'Or what if she does have sex with him, but she's learned her lesson from what happened with Samuel and she makes sure he uses a condom?'

I'd thought about both of those things, too. Becca wasn't stupid; we all knew that. With Ryan, that first time, she'd been unlucky. Too young and inexperienced and scared to be the one to take charge and talk about contraception, and she was caught out. Unlucky. But since then, with Ryan, she'd been more careful. What were the chances of her failing to use protection with Anthony? They seemed ultra slim, to me.

'I don't know,' Lucy said in answer, and I realised we'd been silent, thinking, since Thomas asked his desperate questions. 'Can you use your Chance to help with that, somehow?'

We were all quiet again. All thinking it through, I'm sure. But whoever Thomas inhabited, it didn't seem like there would be an easy way to ensure his conception. To my mind, the best he could do was to get them together on the right day. After that, it was down to them.

A week after that first date, they went out for a drink. Anthony was heading back to Bristol and it was their last chance to meet up for a while. Becca's dad had Samuel again. He seemed pleased that there was a new man on the scene.

That evening, Becca and Anthony had a couple of beers in a local pub. It was easy, smooth. They talked and laughed and took it in turns to go to the bar, and it just looked very natural. And the more natural it looked, the more miserable I felt. So when the pub door opened and Ryan walked in with his friend Carl, I felt a flutter of excitement. And almost straight away, the guilt followed. This was not good news. Becca was having a nice evening, and this could only ruin it. When she saw him, she froze. Anthony noticed, looked up.

'Oh,' he said.

Becca didn't say anything, just looked down at the table. This was the first time they'd run into each other since the split. Ryan hadn't called or messaged her, hadn't asked her to come back. Hadn't asked to see Samuel, either.

Ryan said to Carl that he was going to the toilet, and I saw at once that he was going to have to walk past the table where they were sitting.

'Do you want to go?' Anthony asked.

But it was too late. Ryan stopped when he saw them. 'Wow,' he said.

Becca looked up. Met his gaze.

'You didn't waste any time, did you?' he asked.

He was on the way to being drunk, his voice a little slurred, his steps not quite straight.

'Ryan...' Becca said, and then she stopped.

What was she going to say, or ask? Please don't make a scene? Please just let me go?

'What?' he asked. He moved closer to the table, took a long look at Anthony. 'Who is this guy, anyway?'

'This is Anthony. We were at school together.'

'And who's looking after my son? Or is that a secret? He does know you have a child, doesn't he?'

Anthony stood up, then. He was a few inches taller than Ryan but skinnier, and he looked like he'd never been in a fight. If things got physical, I didn't like his chances. There was a part of me that wanted Ryan to hit him and insist that Becca and Samuel come home, and I was ashamed of it, but it didn't stop it being there. Whispering.

'I know about Samuel,' Anthony said. 'He's with Becca's dad. Any other questions?'

Ryan sniffed, wiped a hand across his face.

'Ryan,' Carl called from the bar. 'Come on, mate, I've nearly finished my pint.'

'Coming,' he called back. And then he turned and went through the door to the toilets without looking at either of them again.

Becca let out a long breath. 'Can we go?' she asked. 'I'm really sorry. Can we just go for a walk or something?'

Anthony nodded. 'Of course.'

Neither of them said that they wanted to make sure they'd gone before Ryan reappeared, but they got their things together quickly, left their half-full bottles of beer. Out on the street, the sky was pink and the sun was setting.

'Beautiful night,' she said.

Anthony took hold of her hand and they walked past the shops and the library and a few other pubs, not really discussing where they were going.

'I'm sorry about Ryan,' Becca said when they had been walking for ten minutes. 'I'm sorry if he ruined the night.'

Anthony stopped, and so did she, and he turned so they were facing one another and took hold of her face with both hands. 'Becca, stop. It's not your fault. He didn't ruin anything. Here we are, together.'

'I bet you wonder why he and I were ever together, don't you?'

Anthony considered this. 'I do, yes. You just seem so... different.'

Becca laughed, but it sounded bitter. 'My dad can't stand him. I think that was part of it, actually. My parents were splitting up, and I was angry with them. And Ryan was older and he seemed a little, I don't know...'

'Dangerous?' Anthony ventured.

'Kind of. I wanted something drastic to happen, to make them take notice. But I also wanted something that was completely about me. I felt like their break-up was the centre of everything and I wanted to show them that I was still there, to remind them that they had a teenage daughter and I was capable of all those teenage mistakes. It seems so stupid now.'

'No, I think I get it.'

'I got pregnant the night we met. And then it seemed like we should try to make a go of it, for Samuel's sake if nothing else.'

'And what happened? What made you leave him?'

Becca sighed. 'He just wasn't much of a dad. I felt so lonely. It's really hard work, being a mum, and you spend a lot of time on your own. With the baby, I mean, but with no one to talk to. It can send you a bit mad. I wanted some support when he wasn't working, and he just didn't want to do it. He didn't want to give up his nights out with Carl and his time on the Xbox. He was just too young and selfish. I mean, I was too young, too, but I just got on with it, because I didn't have a choice.'

She stopped, and then she looked a bit embarrassed, as if she thought she'd said too much.

'I think you're a great mum,' Anthony said. 'Your face lights up when you talk about Samuel.'

Becca's face turned scarlet. 'Thank you, I...'

I tried to remember whether anyone had said this to her before. Probably her dad had. But from him, she would have just taken it in her stride. From Anthony, it was different.

'I bet she wishes he was Samuel's father,' Lucy said.

I wanted to say something, to argue with her, but what could I say? It was probably true.

'I just feel like I've messed everything up,' Becca said. 'I feel like Samuel deserves better. He should have a settled life, a good family, a home.'

'Don't do that, Becca. He has a good family and a home. You can only do so much. You'll get there.'

Anthony leaned in then, to kiss her, and she closed her eyes and I tried to imagine how she might feel. When the kiss was over, she looked all dreamy and peaceful.

'Can we go somewhere?' she asked. 'To your house, maybe?'

Anthony looked at her, his expression serious. 'Are you sure? I don't want to rush you into anything.'

'You're not rushing me,' Becca said. 'I want to.'

'Okay. My parents are away...'

'Why didn't you say so?' Becca asked, nudging him and laughing.

'Because I didn't want you to think I was trying to get you into bed!'

'But I want you to try to get me into bed,' she said.

'Well, I'm very happy to hear that,' he said.

They carried on walking. Every now and again, Anthony tugged on her hand to show her that they needed to turn. And five minutes later, he was unlocking the door to his house and ushering Becca inside.

'I really like you,' Becca said as he closed the front door and turned to face her.

'I really like you too.'

She reached under his shirt and put her hands flat on his chest, then moved them to his back. She kissed him, long and hard. After a couple of minutes, he pulled away and led her by the hand up the stairs and into his bedroom.

I turned to look at Lucy and Thomas. They were smiling, focused. I started to say something, about how it didn't mean anything. But I wasn't sure why. Why did I want to take this away from Thomas? It wasn't my turn yet. It was his. And things were heading in the right direction.

When they had shrugged off their clothes and got into Anthony's single bed, Becca asked if he had a condom and he nodded, reaching into a bedside drawer.

I caught Thomas's eye by mistake, and he looked a little upset, like this was putting a spanner in the works of his great plan. And it was, wasn't it? It might not be his day just yet, but this was setting a precedent.

The sex was different to how it had been with Ryan. Slower, gentler. They moved around, touched each other everywhere, trying to work out how they fit together and what they both liked, and there was a lot of laughter. With Ryan, it had always been silent. Sometimes some music on in the background, but no talking. No laughing. It was good to see her looking relaxed and happy, but it was hard, too.

Afterwards, they lay wrapped around each other, the sheets covering the bottom half of their bodies.

'What now?' Becca asked.

'Right now? I guess we get you home.'

'And later?'

Anthony turned on his side and propped himself up on his elbow. 'What are you asking, Becca Valentine? Are you asking if we're together? Because I'd really like that, if you would.'

And Becca smiled and pulled him towards her for a kiss. 'I'd like that, too.'

14

APRIL 2023

About ten days later, Thomas surprised us.

'I've done it,' he said. 'I've used my Chance.'

I looked at Lucy and saw she was as shocked as I was.

'When?' I asked. 'Why didn't we see?'

'Yesterday,' he said. I thought he seemed a bit smug, about having got something past us. 'You didn't see because Becca wasn't involved. I chose Anthony's friend Luke. Remember, the one who was seeing Ellie for a bit?'

I nodded. I remembered Luke.

'Well,' Thomas went on, 'time is running out and it's looking good, but I wanted to give them an extra nudge. Last time him and Becca spoke on the phone, he said Luke was coming to see him in Bristol. So I made a snap decision and went with it.'

'And?' Lucy asked. 'How did it go? What did you say?'

'I just steered the conversation to Becca a lot, and ended up talking Anthony into taking her away for the weekend which covers my date.'

I was impressed. Lucy looked all lit up.

'That's brilliant,' she said. 'Well done!'

Not for the first time, I wondered how she was feeling about losing him. They'd been a pair, just like Samuel and I had. Did his imminent departure hurt her the way Samuel's had hurt me? She didn't show it. But I didn't know what conversations they had when I wasn't around, or listening. You didn't have to be demonstrative to love deeply. In a short time, it would be just her and me. What would that be like? Thomas was probably the quietest of the four of us, but since Samuel had gone, he'd been a kind of buffer between Lucy and me, keeping things steady and calm. On the other hand, I'd felt like a third wheel in a lot of ways, because of their closeness. It would shake things up, him going.

'What was it like?' I asked.

I'd always been fascinated by how it would be when we used our Chance. The only senses we had were sight and hearing, and I imagined that each other sense would add a layer of depth to the experience of living, but I didn't know what it would be like. I couldn't know.

'I was so nervous,' he said. 'I didn't really take much in. It felt busy, crowded. Lots going on. Luke and Anthony were in a pub and it was loud.'

It wasn't enough. I wanted to know more, but I didn't know how to form the questions.

* * *

When Anthony called to ask Becca to go away with him, we were all expecting it. Thomas was glowing. Becca smiled at the sound of Anthony's voice. It was a Wednesday. Thomas's conception date was the coming Sunday.

'Do you want to come away with me?' Anthony asked. 'You and Samuel, I mean.'

Becca furrowed her brow. 'Away?' she asked. 'Away where?'

'I fancy a trip to the seaside. Maybe Bournemouth? Did you know that George Harrison wrote his first Beatles song in Bournemouth?'

'I didn't,' Becca said. 'I don't even know what his first Beatles song was.'

'"Don't Bother Me". Anyway, the weather forecast for Saturday looks great. I missed your birthday and I want to make it up to you. I could come home tomorrow, skip my Friday lecture, and then we could get the train. I could book us somewhere to stay for a couple of nights. And... Becca. I don't want you to think I'm trying to rush you into anything serious. I'd just really like to spend the weekend with you and your little boy, at the beach. That's it.'

Becca smiled wide. She hadn't had a holiday for a long time. The year before the pregnancy, before her parents had split up, they'd been to Tenerife for a week, the three of them, their little family. But that seemed like a lifetime ago to me, and I was sure it did to Becca too. A weekend away wasn't quite the same as a holiday, but it was something. It was more than Ryan had ever offered.

'I'd really like that,' she said.

'This is it,' Thomas said. 'This is it!'

'Fingers crossed he forgets to take any condoms with him,' Lucy said.

At that, Thomas's face clouded over. This was the one sticking point that Thomas hadn't been able to address with his intervention. All he could do now was wait and see.

'Thomas,' I said. 'Do you think she's ready to have another baby?'

'What do you mean?' There was an edge to his voice and Lucy warned me with her expression to drop this. But I couldn't. I wouldn't.

'I mean, she's just turned nineteen. She already has one small child. She's given up her education. And now she's met the right guy, one who's kinder to her. But he's away at university. Wouldn't it be better, for her, I mean, for them, if they didn't get pregnant right now?'

'But it's my time,' Thomas said, as if he genuinely didn't understand what I was suggesting.

'It's not fair to do that,' Lucy said. 'We're just supposed to do our best to make sure we're conceived. We're not supposed to get into the ethics of whether or not it's the right thing.'

This was what Sarah and Charles had always told us. It's a battle to survive. Do whatever it takes. But back then, I hadn't envisaged things getting so complicated.

'Do you think it's the right thing?' Thomas asked.

Lucy took a while to start speaking. 'I don't know, Thomas. Who can say? None of us can see the future. But if we weren't supposed to at least have a chance, why would we be here at all? There must be a reason why you're here, waiting like this.'

I wasn't so sure about that. I thought it was more random. But I sensed that my views wouldn't be welcomed.

'I think we're programmed to do everything we can,' Thomas said. 'And I won't be made to feel guilty about it.'

There was nothing to be said after that.

* * *

When they were on the train on Friday afternoon, Becca couldn't stop grinning.

'It will be Sammy's first time at the seaside,' she said.

Anthony took hold of her hand. 'Then we'd better make the most of it,' he said.

They were sitting in special seats, opposite the pushchair space, where Samuel's buggy was parked. They looked at Samuel. He was chewing on a breadstick, completely at ease.

'I don't know why I've never thought to take him anywhere like this,' Becca said. 'I always thought the journey would be impossible, with stairs and escalators and all that. But it's been so easy. I feel silly.'

Anthony frowned. 'Don't feel like that. Christ, I wouldn't have wanted to undertake it on my own. It's just easier with someone else, isn't it?'

Ryan was there like a wedge between them, not mentioned but definitely considered in this back and forth they were having. Anthony was probably thinking that Ryan should have done something like this with them. Becca was probably comparing the two men, and I knew which one would be found wanting. For the hundredth time, I wondered whether there was a way to get the two of them back together in the future. Whether I stood a chance, against Lucy.

* * *

On Saturday, they ate a huge breakfast at the hotel. Samuel had a banana followed by a bit of Becca's sausage and eggs and finally a piece of toast with chocolate spread.

'It's the first time he's had chocolate,' Becca said.

'I think it's safe to say he's a fan,' Anthony said.

Samuel was beaming, the skin around his mouth brown and sticky. Anthony leaned in with a wipe he'd pulled from the pack Becca always had with her and wiped away the chocolate while Samuel batted at his hand.

'What do you say about a trip to the beach, little man?'

They bought a cheap bucket and spade at a seaside shop. Anthony took over pushing the buggy when they got onto the sand and it was hard going. And once they'd set themselves up with their blanket laid out and shoes and bags weighing down the corners, Becca lifted Samuel out and plonked him down on the sand. He wriggled a little, put his hand down flat, then lifted it to his mouth and began to lick it. Becca and Anthony reached out at the same time to stop him, and they both laughed. It was refreshing, I noticed, that Anthony was watching. Ryan had rarely paid attention like this, and Samuel was his son. I knew Lucy and Thomas would be thinking along the same lines. I didn't look at them, didn't want to see their smugness.

'This is a perfect day,' Becca announced when they were eating the sandwiches they'd bought on the walk from the hotel.

'Really?' Anthony asked. He was squinting in the spring sun. He'd forgotten his sunglasses. 'But it's nothing special, is it?'

Becca looked like she couldn't believe what he was saying. 'It's so special. Special doesn't have to be expensive or something one of a kind. It's about who you're with.'

They both grinned, and Anthony leaned across the blanket to kiss her, and Samuel looked up at the two of them, too young to understand that this man might just be about to become his stepdad. That he might be on the cusp of having a brother.

The three of them, there on that beach, seemed more like a family than Becca and her parents ever had. Or Becca, Ryan and Samuel, for that matter. And all of a sudden it struck me that biology didn't matter as much as love.

After lunch, Anthony shook the sand from the blanket

and Becca slid Samuel back into the buggy. They went back to the hotel, where Becca put Samuel down for his nap. He was sleeping beside the bed in the travel cot the hotel had provided, his breathing steady. The room was quiet. Becca and Anthony were tiptoeing around, trying not to disturb him. Anthony went up behind her and caught her round the waist and pulled her gently onto the bed, and they started kissing.

'Are you absolutely sure tomorrow is your date?' Lucy asked.

Thomas didn't say anything, just looked at her. We all understood. You didn't forget your date. It was always on your mind, etched in your thoughts. There was no way of getting it wrong.

Anthony and Becca had sex. As expected, Anthony reached into his rucksack for a packet of condoms. I could feel Thomas's fear, but there was nothing any of us could do.

* * *

They went back to the beach, after Samuel's nap. Anthony built sandcastles with Samuel – or for him, rather – and Becca took him for a very quick paddle in the sea. The weather, as expected, was clear and they kept saying how warm it was for April, but the squeals they made suggested that the water was cold. In the late afternoon, they found somewhere to eat and Samuel had a boiled egg and soldiers while Becca and Anthony ate juicy-looking burgers. They had an early night, all of them. Once they'd put Samuel down, they couldn't leave the hotel room and they couldn't make much noise. They drank a couple of beers, sitting on the bed, and then they got under the covers and held one another until holding led to kissing and kissing led to sex. Again, the box of condoms came out. This time, Thomas stayed quiet.

I didn't watch over them all night. I thought about how I'd say goodbye to him. We hadn't always seen eye to eye, but he was my brother. And from the next day onwards, it would be just Lucy and me, and I thought that might be very strange. Lonely, even. We had Becca to watch, of course, but we couldn't interact with her, only with each other, and things had felt tense and taut between us since she'd revealed her true conception date to me.

In the morning, they lay in bed for a long time. Samuel lay between them and kicked his legs, and it struck me again how much they looked and behaved like a family.

'Where's Thomas?' I asked.

'Gone,' Lucy said. She sounded happy and sad.

'Gone? When?'

'In the night. A little after midnight, they woke up and had sex again, and he disappeared.'

I felt stupid. Of course Sunday started in the middle of the night. I'd just assumed it would be later. I would have stayed up with them, if I'd known. I would have said the things I wanted to say to him.

'So what about the condom thing?' I asked.

'It tore,' Lucy said. 'Anthony realised, afterwards, and they talked about getting the morning-after pill today. We have to make sure that doesn't happen.'

'How?' I asked.

'I'm going to use my Chance. Talk her out of it or something.'

I didn't know what to say. There was no rule, I supposed, that said you had to use your Chance for your own good. It was selfless of her to even think of using hers like this. And if she did, it would change the footing between us again, wouldn't it? Her with the dad Becca was more likely to stay with, but me with the chance to step into their world and do something to make my conception happen.

'Were you with him?' I asked, changing the subject. 'At the end?'

'Of course.'

She didn't ask why I wasn't, but the words hung in the air between us regardless, and they felt like an accusation.

'I thought... I didn't think of the early hours of the morning. I thought it would be today, or tonight. I thought I'd get a chance to say goodbye.'

Lucy didn't say anything. I'd hoped she might reassure me, tell me that he'd known the way I felt, but she didn't. She couldn't, could she? Because even I hadn't known. Part of me had wanted him to be conceived, part of me hadn't. And I would never love him the way I loved Samuel.

'What did you two talk about, while you waited?' I asked.

Lucy paused before speaking. 'I told him I loved him, that I couldn't wait to be with him again.'

That confidence she had, that she would definitely get to be with him in the future, really stung. She must have known it would. I felt bereft. Lucy was the only person in my world and it was clear that she was furious with me. I turned to Becca and Anthony, who were starting to get up.

'What's on the agenda for today, other than going home?' Becca asked.

She looked a little downcast at the thought of heading back, and I could imagine that she wished they could live in this seaside bubble forever, just the three of them. But life just wasn't like that.

'I thought we could go out for a big breakfast and then have a look around the shops,' Anthony said. 'The train's at one o'clock.'

'Sounds good,' Becca said. She went into the bathroom to shower, and when she came out, Anthony had changed and dressed Samuel and packed up most of their things.

They'd only just left the hotel when they passed a pharmacy and Anthony caught hold of Becca's arm and asked if they should go in. Without knowing I was going to do it, I went up close to Becca and tried to communicate with her. *Don't go in, don't go in, don't go in.* She looked unsure.

'Should I do it now?' Lucy asked, seeming panicked. 'Should I go there, and be Becca, and not get the pill at all? Or should I just stop her from taking it later?'

'Give me a minute,' I said. I concentrated hard. I thought of Thomas, of the Thomas I'd known and the Thomas I might know again, the one who might become Samuel's baby brother, who might be the starting point of a happier life for Becca.

Don't go in, I thought. *Don't go in.*

Becca had stopped on the street. She was leaning on the pushchair, and Anthony was waiting patiently for her response.

'You know what, I'm sure it's okay,' Becca said. 'I just had my period last week.'

Lucy smiled, looked at me with a question in her eyes.

'Are you sure?' Anthony asked.

'Yes,' she said. 'Come on, we only have a few hours left. Let's make the most of them.'

I felt elated and exhausted. It did something to you, that depth of concentration. It wiped you out.

'Did you do that?' Lucy asked. 'For him? For me?'

'For her,' I said. 'For them.' And we both looked at Becca, at the way she was walking, as if she was lighter than she'd been for a long time.

15

MAY 2023

For a month, Lucy and I waited – mostly in silence – for Becca to realise she was pregnant. And while we waited, something unexpected happened. Ryan called.

It was a Saturday afternoon and Becca was wandering the streets with the buggy, trying to get Samuel to have his afternoon nap. When she pulled her phone from her pocket, we all saw his name displayed on the screen, and while Lucy laughed a little scornfully, I felt a flutter of excitement. I wondered which was closer to the way Becca felt.

'Hi?' she said.

She said it casually, as if she was expecting him to announce that he'd called by mistake. We crowded in so that we could make out his side of the conversation.

'Hi, Becca. Can I see you? You and Sammy?'

This was unexpected. The surprise was written all over her face, not just in her eyes and her mouth, but in the creases in her forehead as she frowned, too.

'Why, Ryan? What do you want?'

'I miss you,' he said. 'I want you back.'

It was too late for this, wasn't it? Things with Anthony were good and, though she didn't know it yet, there was a new life beginning inside her that was part her and part him. It seemed unlikely that there was a space for Ryan anywhere in all of that. I looked at Lucy. She was trying to pretend she wasn't terrified, but I could see right through it. Not a single one of us had anticipated this.

'Ryan, I'm with someone else...'

It was a protest, but not a strong one. She could have told him it was too late, or said she had no desire to see him again, but she didn't. It sounded almost like she wanted him to persuade her.

'I'm Sammy's dad, Becca,' Ryan said. 'Don't you think we owe it to him to at least try?'

That was probably his strongest card. I was riveted to Becca's face, wondering how she would respond.

'Look,' Ryan said. 'That night in the pub, I'd had a few drinks, I shouldn't have talked to you both like that. But really, Becca, what can he give you that I can't?'

'Love, respect, kindness,' Lucy whispered.

'And isn't he away at uni? He's not going to throw all that away to settle down with you and my son, is he?'

This was a sore point. It had come up a couple of times. Anthony wanted them to enjoy the moment, just be happy to be together and not worry so much about the future. But Becca argued that she wasn't in a position to do that. She had a child, and she had to think about what was going to happen to them, and plan things, and it wasn't fair of him to make her sound like she was nagging for trying to do so.

'What do you know about all that?' Becca asked, her anger tight and coiled.

'It doesn't matter,' Ryan said. 'It's true, isn't it? I'm here,

Becca. I'm here, and I'm not going anywhere. And more importantly, I'm Sammy's dad. Think about it.'

And then he was gone, and Becca paused in the middle of the pavement with people rushing all around her, until Samuel started kicking his legs, asking to get moving again.

* * *

That night, Becca and Anthony were going out with some of his friends. He was spending most of his weekends at home so he could see Becca, but this get-together with old school friends had been planned for months, and he'd invited Becca to join them. Becca didn't say anything to Anthony about Ryan's call when she arrived at the pub. He was already there with three or four people.

'Do you think she'll tell him later?' I asked Lucy.

If I'd had anyone else to ask, I would have done. But I didn't.

'No, because she's going to ignore it,' Lucy said.

I wasn't sure whether she was confident or not. Her voice seemed sort of shaky, and it was as if she was trying to convince herself.

'Hey,' Anthony said, standing and kissing Becca on the lips. 'Do you remember Luke and Sophie? And Mohammed?'

I stared at Sophie until I could make them out. Three Almosts hovering nearby. Two boys and a girl. We smiled at each other but didn't say anything.

Becca looked around the group. 'Hi,' she said, and they all nodded to her and lifted their glasses. The time when Luke had been with Ellie seemed like a different life.

Anthony went to the bar to get Becca a drink.

'Anthony hasn't told us much about you,' Sophie said. 'You went to our school, didn't you?'

'Yes,' Becca said. 'I was a year below.'

'Are you at uni now?' Sophie pressed.

'No, I— I had a baby.'

Becca had said this many times, but it didn't seem to get easier. The reactions she got were varied. Sometimes, people seemed shocked. Sometimes, embarrassed. If Sophie felt either of those things, she hid it well. 'And what do you do now?' she asked.

'I'm just a mum,' Becca said.

That 'just' made me so sad, it was like a physical ache.

'Although I'd like to get back into education when my little boy is a bit older,' Becca added.

I wasn't sure whether that was true or whether she just felt like she had to say it, in this company. She was shifting in her chair, uncomfortable. She kept looking over to the bar to see whether Anthony was coming back. But he had his back to her, and he hadn't ordered yet.

'What about you?' Becca asked.

'I'm at Bristol with Anthony.'

'Do you think there's something going on with them?' Lucy asked, horrified.

I had wondered the same thing, but Anthony didn't seem like the type who would see two girls at the same time, much less bring them together on the same evening. No, I was sure there was nothing. But that didn't mean Sophie didn't want there to be.

Becca didn't seem to know what to say next, and she started to bite on a fingernail. Sophie took a sip from her glass of wine.

The other two at the table had their heads close together. They were discussing a film, from what I could gather, but they didn't attempt to draw Sophie or Becca in. A couple of minutes passed in painful silence before Anthony returned with two bottles of beer and a glass of wine balanced in his hands. He passed the wine to Sophie, and she smiled and finished off the glass she was drinking.

'What have I missed?' Anthony asked.

Neither of the girls said anything.

A little later, when Becca had had four beers, she leaned across to Anthony when Sophie was in the toilets.

'I didn't know Sophie was at Bristol too,' Becca said.

'Yes,' Anthony said.

'Did she go there because of you?'

'No,' Anthony said, slowly and precisely. 'She went there because it's a really good university and they do the course she wanted to study.'

Becca said nothing. She was out of her depth. The conversation turned, again and again, to politics, or history, or inside jokes from uni. Anthony kept trying to get her involved, but each time she faltered and took an exit by going to the bar or the toilet as quickly as she could. She looked like she'd had enough.

'Can we go?' she asked.

Anthony screwed his face up. 'Come on, Becca. It's only nine thirty, and I don't get to see these guys very often.'

I wanted her to say that she would be up early with Samuel, while he could sleep in with a hangover. I wanted her to say that surely he could see Sophie whenever he wanted, since they were living in the same city and studying at the same university. But she didn't.

'Fine, I'll go,' she said.

'I'm not going to let you walk home alone at this time,' Anthony said, reaching for his coat.

'You're not going to *let* me?' Becca asked, her voice quiet but sharp as glass.

Sophie was squeezing back into her seat and looked from one to the other of them, and then away.

'You know what I mean,' Anthony said. He looked at the others. 'We're going to make a move...'

'No,' Becca said, standing. 'You stay. I'm going. It was nice to meet you all.'

She got up and walked away without looking back.

'He'll go after her,' Lucy said, and I wondered who she was trying to convince. But she was right – he did. He caught her by the arm when she was a few metres away from the door.

'Becca,' he said, and the way he said it, it was like a plea.

'I'm not part of that world,' Becca said.

Anthony looked stunned, like he'd been expecting more back and forth about staying and going.

'I don't fit there,' she went on. 'It's partly because I had a baby instead of going to university, but it's more than that, too. They're all so comfortable in what they know and understand, and they're confident that life will be easy for them. They might be wrong, but it doesn't matter for now. I just can't be like that. You're like it too, and I thought it was charming. I still do. But less so now I see it's just part of being in that crowd, with all that privilege.'

'What are you talking about?' Anthony asked. He was still holding onto her arm, and they both looked down at where their bodies were touching. 'It doesn't have to be complicated. They're just my friends, and I wanted them to meet you, because I like you. I really like you, Becca Valentine.'

'Why do you always do that? Say my full name like that?'

He looked hurt. 'I just... I thought it was sort of our thing.'

'I need to go home,' Becca said. 'And I don't need you to walk me, honestly. I'm fine. Go back in and enjoy your night with your friends.'

Anthony looked like he didn't know what to do. He was a gentleman. It wasn't in his nature to let a woman wander off into the night. But he wasn't pushy either and she'd made it clear she wanted him to let her go. So in the end, he turned and went back inside the pub. But not before watching her walk away, the look in his eyes a little sad, a little lost.

When Becca got to the fork in Clarendon Street, where the right road would take her home, she took the left.

'No!' Lucy shouted.

I didn't say anything, but I felt a rush of anticipation. She was going to Ryan's. When she got to the flat, she stood for a long minute outside before pushing the buzzer. And when Ryan opened the door, she didn't go in straight away, even though he gestured for her to do so.

'I'm not promising anything...' she said.

Ryan smiled. He knew that it was done. That he had her.

'Come on,' he said. 'I'm letting all the heat out.'

And she stepped inside.

16

MAY 2023

She told Anthony the next day. She didn't leave him hanging, and I admired her for that. Lucy was furious.

'It's the most ridiculous decision,' she said. 'Why would anyone give up someone who cares about her and treats her well to be with someone like him?'

I said nothing. It was obvious, wasn't it? It was what Ryan had said, about being Samuel's dad and about being there. Anthony was going places. Not just the years in Bristol for university. He wasn't likely to stay in their town and Becca knew it. When she'd made the decision to keep Samuel, Becca had tied herself to a certain kind of life with a certain kind of man. Or at least, she felt she had. And I was inclined to agree.

She met Anthony for a coffee in town, told him she was moving back in with Ryan. He screwed up his face in a way that reminded me so much of Lucy, I almost laughed out loud.

'Why?' he asked. 'I really thought things were going well for us, and Ryan, well, he's...'

What was he? It was clear that Anthony didn't know how to finish that sentence, at least in a way that would be polite.

'He's Sammy's dad,' Becca said. 'That's the bottom line.'

Anthony nodded, then. There was no arguing with that. And perhaps he'd been starting to wonder how it was going to work, too. His big plans weren't going away, and neither was her son. Their lives weren't compatible.

'And it's not just that. We're living totally different lives, and liking each other isn't going to be enough, in the end. You should be enjoying your time in Bristol, not coming home to see me every weekend. And I think Sophie has a thing for you.'

Anthony shook his head, started to protest.

'I'm not saying anything's been going on, just that it might, in the future. She's much more your kind of girl.'

Lucy shouted, 'Tell her *she's* your kind of girl!' But he didn't. He didn't say anything else about it. He just drained his coffee cup and stood up, and he left. And a couple of minutes later, Becca pushed the buggy out onto the street, struggling a little to keep both doors open at the same time to allow for the width of it. And it felt like a metaphor for her life.

When Becca told her dad she was moving back in with Ryan, he let out a long sigh.

'Are you sure?' he asked her. 'What's changed?'

'He's going to try,' Becca said. 'That's all anyone can do, really, isn't it?'

'You know you'll always have a home here, if you need it.'

Becca looked as if she was about to speak again, and I thought she was probably going to say that she didn't need it, wouldn't. That things were going to work out for them this time. But then she didn't say anything, so perhaps she wasn't that sure of herself, after all.

She went upstairs to her room after that conversation, and she cried. Great heaving sobs. Samuel was napping in the travel cot beside her bed, and it was clear that she was trying not to make too much noise. Did she want to avoid waking him or make sure her dad didn't hear? Probably a bit of both. But I hated the fact that she was sad, and on her own, and trying to keep quiet.

'Why is she doing this when it makes her so sad?' Lucy asked.

But I didn't answer, because I knew she wasn't really asking me. People did this kind of thing, I'd observed. Made decisions that didn't always seem like the right ones. Did things that made them sad. They were always doing it. It could be baffling. But in this instance, I thought it was about what she expected for herself, what she thought she deserved. And also, a little, about the fact that her parents had broken up her family and she'd made a new family to replace it and she wanted to fight for that family to stay together. I think she believed that that's what would make her a good mum. From a selfish perspective, I couldn't help but be pleased it was going this way, no matter how much I hated to see Becca in such a state.

A few hours later, when she turned up at Ryan's flat with two suitcases full of hers and Samuel's belongings, you wouldn't have known she'd been crying unless you looked really closely. And Ryan didn't. He pulled her inside and kissed her, and it was the kind of kiss he'd given her in the early days, before Samuel. He gestured for her to put the suitcases down in the hallway and he guided her into the bedroom. The bed was unmade, and the way Becca wrinkled her nose made me think it must have smelled. This had been her home, I reminded myself. Their home. She would make it work.

Ryan pushed her down on the bed, playfully, and got on top of her. Becca laughed but she looked unsure.

'What about all my things?' she said.

He gave a little shrug and kissed her again, and I saw his

tongue slide into her mouth. How did that feel? It looked like a violation, an intrusion. But she didn't seem to mind. Pretty soon, their clothes were tangled on the floor and he was pushing himself inside her, and there was a look in her eyes that I couldn't pin down. That I didn't like.

After he was finished, Ryan held her. They lay on their sides, his arm thrown over her and resting on her hip.

'You know, you still have some baby weight to lose,' he said.

Becca froze. Her body still, her face crumpling. 'It's not that easy,' she said.

Ryan laughed. 'It's been almost a year.'

In spite of myself, I was furious on her behalf. I exchanged a look with Lucy, and it was loaded. *See*, she was saying, *he's no good. He's no good for her*. I looked away first.

Becca shuffled out of his arms and sat on the edge of the bed, pulling her clothes back on.

'Are you in a mood now?' Ryan asked.

He was behind Becca and couldn't see her expression, but I could. It was humiliation.

'No, I just need to get on. Dad's got Samuel. Can you drive me over there to pick up some more of our things?'

Ryan pulled on his boxers and a T-shirt. 'Okay,' he said. But he didn't make a move to put his jeans on. For a few minutes, they moved around one another, not speaking. And then Becca caved.

'Please, Ryan,' she said. 'I really need to get back there.'

And Ryan said nothing, but he reached for his jeans. He was smiling.

* * *

By early evening, it was done, and the three of them were in Ryan's flat with bags and boxes all around them.

'I'm sure you didn't have this much stuff before,' Ryan said, looking around. 'How the hell are we supposed to fit it all in?'

'Too late to change your mind now,' Becca said.

I could see what she was doing. She was trying to give as good as she got. To show that she wasn't offended by his offensive remarks, which were supposed to be jokes but weren't really funny. But I could see that they were affecting her, that each one was like a pin stuck in her delicate skin.

Samuel had recently started walking around holding onto the furniture, and he kept getting into places he shouldn't, courting danger. And each time, Becca hauled him back to her. She was putting his cot together, pushing her hair out of her eyes. She found a bag of his toys, upended it on the floor of the bedroom and he was delighted. But within minutes, he was trying to climb a pile of boxes again.

'This is hopeless,' Becca said. 'Can you watch him while I finish this?'

Ryan put his head round the door of the bedroom. 'Come on, little man,' he said, picking Samuel up and taking him through to the living room.

'Thank you,' Becca said, and I wished I could tell her she didn't have to. That they were partners in this, that Samuel was just as much Ryan's responsibility as her own. But it didn't feel like that, and I wondered whether it ever would.

When Becca emerged from the bedroom, the cot made, she found Ryan and Samuel sitting side by side on the sofa, watching football on TV. It wasn't the way she looked after him. She played and talked to him and showed him things. But this was how it was, with Ryan, and she'd known that. He hadn't changed into a different person in the time they'd been apart.

'Shall we get a takeaway tonight?' she asked, sitting down on the sofa next to them.

'Thing is, I haven't got any money until payday. Have you?'

I knew that Becca had some money, mostly given to her by her dad. I hoped she wouldn't spend it on a takeaway. She shook her head and then went over to the kitchen area, opened the cupboard.

'Beans on toast?' she suggested.

Ryan made a sound that might have been agreement, and Becca got out a pan and the tin. She looked weary. I wanted to look away, but couldn't. Was this how it was going to be, forever? Was she just taking on another person to look after, without getting anything for herself in return? I reminded myself that Ryan was my dad, too. That I was invested in them staying together and making it work. Perhaps things would get better. They were so young. Both of them feeling their way, unsure how relationships and parenting actually worked.

That night in bed, Ryan reached out for Becca and she pushed his hand away.

'Not now,' she whispered.

Ryan looked annoyed but he didn't say anything. He turned his back to Becca and pulled the covers over himself until they were barely covering her. And within a couple of minutes, he was snoring. It was a muffled, low sound, surely not enough to keep Becca awake. And yet she lay there for a good hour or more, eyes wide, body still, looking from her boyfriend to their baby now and again. I wished I knew what she was thinking. Had she made a mistake? And if she had, was it undoable?

When her phone buzzed, she reached out to silence it, but Ryan hadn't stirred. It was a message from Anthony. It read:

Are you sure, Becca Valentine?

She deleted it and put the phone back on the floor next to the bed. And then she cried, steady and silent. Finally, long after midnight, her eyelids drooped and her breathing slowed and she slept peacefully until Sammy awoke, as he always did, sometime after five o'clock in the morning. And then, bleary-eyed, she pulled him from his cot and took him into the living room while Ryan slept on, apparently oblivious. It was a new day.

* * *

The next couple of weeks were tough for all of us. Becca was trying to find her way, trying to fit herself and Samuel back into that space, which had once been part theirs but had somehow become more masculine and unwelcoming in their absence. There were arguments, some of them bitter, but most of them over quickly. At least once a day, no matter how things were between them, Ryan tried to initiate sex, and more often than not, Becca pulled away. And I had to wonder what had made her go back, if this was how she felt.

It seemed like they were in a stalemate, and nothing was going to change. But I knew, of course, that it would. That she would find out, at some point, that she was carrying Thomas. And then she'd have some decisions to make.

17

JUNE 2023

Weeks went by before Becca finally took a test. She hadn't said anything to anyone, but I wondered whether she'd known for a while and just hadn't been able to face it. Or perhaps she was waiting until a time when she could conceivably believe that the baby's father was the man she was living with, and not the man she'd left behind. Lucy and I watched her as she waited for the test to show her future. And when it did, she muttered something under her breath and went on with her day. Did she know? Did she know for sure that the baby was Anthony's? She hadn't used one of those tests that told you how many weeks you were. Just the kind that told you 'yes' or 'no'.

Ryan came home late that night, after going for a few drinks with the men he worked with, and he was in a better mood than usual, making jokes and touching Becca's hair. Samuel was already asleep, and Becca had made a shepherd's pie.

'I need to talk to you about something,' she said, once he'd taken off his shoes and coat.

Lucy looked at me. Neither of us had expected her to do it,

at least not so soon, but she must have decided that there was no better time.

Ryan sat down on the sofa and put his arm around her. 'What's up, babe?'

The oven was humming, the baby monitor was on the coffee table. It was a little too quiet in the flat.

'I'm pregnant,' Becca said.

Ryan didn't lift his arm or get angry, like I'd thought he might. He just laughed. It was loud but not unkind. 'Pregnant?'

Becca nodded.

'Well, I wasn't expecting that!'

'Are you pleased?' Becca asked.

'I suppose so! Two kids, Jesus, but why not?'

His reaction was such a stark contrast to last time, and Becca looked as surprised as I felt. But last time, they'd been little more than strangers, and now, they were already a family, so it made sense in that respect. There was a small part of me, though, that kept going back to the split. To how easily he'd let them go.

'What about you, babe? Aren't you happy?'

Becca smiled a little. 'I am,' she said.

The smile didn't reach her eyes, but if she was wondering whether going ahead with the pregnancy was the right thing, she didn't bring it up. I waited for Ryan to realise how soon this had happened after them getting together. To start asking questions. But he didn't. And she didn't bring it up, of course. And unexpectedly, the evening turned into a kind of celebration.

* * *

For the next couple of weeks, Ryan stepped up. He took Becca a cup of tea in bed every morning and he helped out more with

Samuel when he was at home. Becca's morning sickness lasted all day, and she often had to put the TV on to entertain Samuel while she kneeled beside the toilet bowl and retched in the middle of the afternoon. They got used to the idea of being a family of four, and Lucy and I got used to it, too. We were remembering how it had been to miss Samuel for those nine months, and then for him to appear, different but the same in some fundamental way, still ours. We missed Thomas, of course we did, but we trusted in the way it all worked, now. We knew that he wasn't lost to us. That we would see him again, and then see him every day as he made his way through his early years.

And Samuel would have a brother! We were all excited about that. About how he'd react, how they would love and protect one another. Of course, Becca and Ryan didn't know whether it would be a boy or a girl. When they talked about names for both, when the name Eliza came up, I couldn't help but be excited. Not this time, I wanted to whisper to them. But soon.

In the middle of all this, Samuel turned one. Becca and Ryan invited their parents and a few friends with babies to come to their flat. It was crowded, but it was a bright, clear day and they had the patio door open and people spilled out onto the small garden. They'd brought presents wrapped in primary coloured paper and bottles of wine and beer. Ryan drank too much and kept whispering in Becca's ear, and she kept pushing him away, a secret smile on her face. He wanted to tell everyone about the new baby, I guessed, and she wasn't sure. Didn't want to tempt fate. Samuel was in heaven, passed from person to person from the moment he woke from his post-lunch nap. Handed presents and cake.

Becca's dad put his arms around her when people were starting to drift away.

'I'm really proud of you,' he said. 'It's not easy, having a child. You're doing such a good job of it. He's a great little man.'

I thought perhaps Becca wanted him to acknowledge that it wasn't all her doing, that Ryan was a part of this little unit too, but she didn't say anything.

'Thanks, Dad,' she said, colouring a little.

'It will get easier as he gets a bit older,' her dad continued. 'And then you'll be able to go to uni or get a job or something. I'll help out, if I can. This first year is the hardest.'

Becca smiled a little stiffly. She put a hand to her stomach, which was the same size as usual, for now, and then she moved it to her hip. And the next time Ryan whispered to her, she was firmer.

'Not today,' I heard her hiss at him. 'Today's about Samuel. We'll do it after the scan.'

Becca's mum spent most of the afternoon looking uncomfortable. She'd been to the flat two or three times, but it always seemed like she was doing it out of duty. She'd bring something for Samuel, but she never got down on the floor to play with him. Becca seemed to have accepted that that was how it was going to be. That day, Liz talked to Dave a little, and to Ryan's mum, but she didn't look like she fitted anywhere. She hovered around, going to the toilet too often and drinking a bit too much wine.

'Mum,' Becca said, approaching her, 'thanks for coming.'

She didn't say 'Of course I would come' or 'It's my grandson's birthday' or 'There's nowhere I'd rather be'. She said, 'Well.'

The two of them stood side by side, watching Samuel. He was holding onto the coffee table and had pulled himself up to standing. He would take his first steps any day, I thought. That's what everyone said, when they saw him.

'He'll be a handful, when he starts walking,' her mum said.

'He's a handful now.'

'Just you wait.'

'Mum, I...'

Becca's mum turned to face her daughter and nodded to encourage Becca to continue.

'I'm okay, you know. We're okay. I know you don't think much of Ryan but he takes care of us. We're fed and warm.'

Her mum shook her head. 'Oh, Becca, fed and warm isn't such a high standard. Your dad and me wanted more for you than this.'

'Like what you have?' Becca asked, and then she walked away without waiting for an answer.

* * *

A week later, Becca ran into Ellie in town. It was like a reunion, because it had been so long since they'd seen each other, which made it a happy occasion marked with hugs and big smiles, but the very fact that it had been so long made it kind of awkward, too. Ellie was at university by then, still living at home but commuting into London for lectures. The two of them had drifted apart, as I'd expected.

'Are you finished for the summer?' Becca asked.

And I wondered whether she was thinking that that might mean Anthony was home.

'Yes, I had my end-of-year exams last week. Do you have time for a proper chat?' Ellie asked.

Becca looked down at the buggy. Samuel was sleeping soundly and was likely to stay that way for another half an hour. 'Yes,' she said. 'Let's get a coffee or something.'

'So what's been going on?' Ellie asked when they'd gone into a café, ordered their drinks and were sitting at a tucked-away table in the corner. 'I heard you were seeing Anthony for a while. I always wanted the two of you to get together!'

It was funny, I thought, how people felt the need to rewrite history. Ellie hadn't always wanted Becca and Anthony to get together. It had been a fleeting thing that had almost happened and then hadn't, quite. I tried to make out the expression on Becca's face. Was she put out? It was hard to tell. Her face remained neutral and she kept her eyes lowered. They'd been such good friends, these two. And then they'd gone in different directions – Becca into motherhood, Ellie into further education – and there had been a few visits but it had been clear from the outset that they would taper off. I tried to remember the last time Ellie had visited the flat, but I couldn't. After she'd stopped visiting, there had been the odd text, the odd call. But nothing much.

'Who did you hear that from?' Becca asked.

Ellie shrugged. 'Oh, I don't know. You know how it is. Stories get around.'

I wondered whether it bothered Becca, that people were obviously talking about her behind her back, making judgements on the choices she was making. If it did, she didn't let it show.

'Ryan and I had a break, things weren't working out, and then I ran into Anthony and we went on a few dates, but it was nothing much.'

It wasn't the truth. It hadn't been nothing much. It had seemed, at the time, like it might just be everything. Perhaps this was the way she had to spin it for herself these days.

'And now?' Ellie asked.

'I've moved back in with Ryan. And we're...'

Becca stopped herself. Was she going to tell Ellie about the baby? It had seemed like she was. If she did, it would be the first time she'd told anyone other than Ryan. It seemed strange that she would choose Ellie for this, her erstwhile friend.

'You're what?' Ellie leaned in closer, and I could see that she was hungry for gossip, for news.

'We... well...' Becca stumbled for a second time and Lucy caught my eye, but I wasn't sure what message she was trying to convey. 'We're having another baby.'

Ellie took a sharp breath in, and Becca looked at her with her eyes wide, and Ellie hastily tried to rearrange her expression into one of neutrality.

'Wow, how old is Sammy now?'

'He's just turned one,' Becca said.

Her words hung in the air as they both silently acknowledged that Ellie should probably have sent a card.

'I can't believe you'll be a mum of two!'

It was the kind of thing people said when they didn't know what to say. It didn't really mean anything. Why couldn't she believe that? What was so unbelievable about it? I was pretty sure that this meeting was a disaster, that the two girls would soon part ways and would never sit down for a chat like this again, so I was astounded when Becca confided in Ellie a second time.

'There's something else,' she said.

Ellie leaned in.

'It's hard to say it. I haven't told anyone...'

Ellie tilted her head slightly to one side. 'Becca, you know me. I won't tell a soul.'

Over the years, they had confided in one another. Boys and school stuff and friendships. Arguments with their parents and embarrassments and fears. Ellie had never let Becca down, as far as I knew. As far as Becca knew. She was trustworthy, or at least she had been. But she wasn't a friend any more, was she? And then I realised, sadly, that Becca didn't really have friends any more. She spent her days with Samuel and Ryan, with her dad. Anthony had been a friend to her, but she'd cut him off when their brief relationship ended. And Ellie had walked away. Perhaps she just needed to talk to someone. Who could blame her for that?

'I don't know for sure, but...' Becca began. 'There's a chance that the baby might be... that it might be Anthony's.'

Ellie took the impact without showing it on her face. 'Does he know?' she asked. 'Anthony, I mean. Well, do either of them know?'

Becca shook her head. 'It's such a mess. It's driving me mad, the worry of it.'

'Whose would you like it to be?' Ellie asked.

Becca's head snapped up. It seemed like she'd never thought to ask herself that. 'Ryan's, of course. He's Sammy's dad, and we're living with him. It has to be him.'

'But it isn't,' Lucy said beside me. Her tone was mocking and I wanted, in that instant, to hurt her. If we'd had real bodies, ones you could touch, I fear I would have hurt her.

'So what are you going to do?' Ellie asked.

'I don't know,' Becca said. 'What can I do?'

Ellie didn't say anything. What were the options, after all? A DNA test, either before or after the birth? But that would involve telling both of the potential fathers, and it was clear that that wasn't really an option. Waiting to see who the baby looked like? It was risky, and there were no guarantees that it would be clear. And if it was, and the answer wasn't the one Becca wanted, the consequences could be severe.

Becca lifted her coffee cup to her lips and drained it. 'Nothing,' she said, in answer to her own question. 'I can't do anything.'

'You need to see Anthony,' Ellie said. 'Tell him. He won't be angry about it the way Ryan will.'

Becca looked up at her friend and I could see that she was mulling it over. I tried to imagine a conversation with Anthony about this, how it would go. It was hard to know, but I was confident of one thing. Ellie was right; Anthony wouldn't get angry. Becca pulled her phone from her pocket and started tapping at it. I didn't have to look to know that she was messaging him. I felt a shiver of worry, of fear. I couldn't say anything to Lucy, because she'd think I was being bitter about the possibility of Anthony coming back on the scene. But I was sure it wasn't just that. Something didn't feel right, and I didn't have to wait long to find out what it was.

18

JULY 2023

'I don't know why I'm here,' Anthony said, running his hands through his shaggy hair.

It was the second time he'd said it, and Becca hadn't really answered the first time.

'You can't do this,' he said, then. 'You can't just keep changing your mind. Going back and forth.'

'That's not what I'm doing,' Becca said.

They were in a café in town, the same café where Becca had sat with Ellie a few days before. It was a Saturday, and her dad had offered to have Samuel for the afternoon. She hadn't wanted to rely on Ryan being helpful. Anthony had taken some persuading to come. He was sitting with an untouched black coffee on the table in front of him. Becca was sipping at a latte.

'Then what are you doing? Do you know how hurt I was when you ended things like that, with no warning? And then I hear from you again, and you want to meet, and you won't tell me why. It's messed up, Becca.'

'I'm pregnant.'

Two words, and all the anger drained from Anthony's face, along with the colour. He reached out a hand.

'Oh, Becca.'

It was as if she'd told him that someone had died. Perhaps that's how he saw it. Becca pulled her hand away from his.

'Is it...?' Anthony started but couldn't finish. And it was such a simple question. I was disappointed in him, and I thought Becca probably was too.

'Yours?' Becca asked, and he nodded awkwardly. 'I don't know for sure.'

'Do you want to keep it?'

'Yes.' This was matter-of-fact, definite. It didn't invite further discussion, and Anthony respected that.

'I can't tell Ryan, you've seen what he's like. And we're living with him again, now, me and Sammy, and it's going okay. So I think it's best if we all just pretend that the baby is definitely his. Which it probably is, right?'

Anthony's face changed and I could see the kindness in it that he'd always shown her before. 'But if— I mean, if that's your plan, to pretend you know it's his...'

'Yes?' Becca asked, looking up, prompting him to go on.

'Then why are you here, telling me about it at all?'

What could she say? That her old friend had thought it was a good idea, that she needed someone to share her story with? That she missed him? It spoke volumes that the man she'd felt able to go to about this predicament was not the one she was sharing her life with. I knew I'd hear more about that from Lucy later, and how could I disagree?

Becca shrugged and she looked fifteen for a moment. There had been a boy, once, when she was fifteen, who she had obsessed over for a year or more. She and Ellie had spent hours shut up in her bedroom talking about him, dissecting every facial expression he'd made, every word he'd spoken. And she'd never once found the nerve to tell him how she felt. How had she gone from that, to this, in such a short time? Her face was harder, now. It was like a mask that she wore, to keep the world at bay. And it only slipped when she was with Anthony.

'I don't know,' Becca said. 'I don't know.'

Anthony reached for his coffee and drained half the cup in one. Becca pushed her latte away. There was silence, and it wasn't awkward, but it wasn't quite comfortable either.

'What do you want me to do? Or say?' Anthony asked. He asked it kindly, showing her that he wasn't angry any more.

'If it was yours,' Becca said. 'If I knew that for sure, what would you want?'

Anthony shook his head a little, as though trying to clear his thoughts.

'I don't want to have a baby, Becca. When we were together, I thought we were in it for the long haul, and I knew Samuel was part of the package, and I was fine with that. More than fine. But this is different. This baby isn't here yet. And I can't lie and say that I want you to have it, that I want us to have it. In the future, I want all that. But not right now.'

I looked across at Lucy and saw that her expression was one of pure devastation. The mention of having a child in the future hadn't reached her, I thought. All she could see was that he didn't want it now. He didn't want Thomas. He wasn't offering to be a family with her.

Becca nodded, as if to say that she understood, and I could see from the almost imperceptible shake of her lips that she didn't trust herself to speak. Sometimes, I'd learned, kindness is the hardest thing to accept.

'If you're sure you want to go ahead with the pregnancy,

then I think what you're suggesting is the right thing,' Anthony went on. 'Stay with Ryan. It sounds like you think the baby is his, anyway.'

Becca nodded again. 'I had to know,' she said.

What did she mean by that? She had to know whether there was a chance for them? Or had to know what his stance on having a child was? I didn't know, and I suspected Anthony didn't either, but he didn't ask. It was clear that she wasn't finding it easy to speak.

'Can I get you home?' Anthony asked.

'No, I'm fine. I can walk,' she said.

They both stood up, and then Anthony stepped forward and pulled her into a hug, and I was reminded of how they fit together, of how happy they'd made one another. I thought they were probably thinking about that too, standing there together, both reluctant to pull away.

'I'm sorry,' she said. 'I'm sorry for how I ended things, and for telling you all this. It was just so clear to me, that night in the pub, that we were going in such different directions.'

'It's okay,' Anthony said. They'd moved outside and he was kicking the toe of his trainer against the concrete paving slabs absent-mindedly. And it was so clearly not okay. It was so clear that there was love there, between them.

'I hope you have a brilliant summer. Then it's your final year.'

'Thanks. I hope you're happy, too, Becca Valentine.'

They walked away in opposite directions, and neither of them looked back. But Becca stopped, after a minute or two, and leaned against a shopfront, and I thought she was going to cry. And I knew she was thinking about what she was doing, about the absolute ridiculousness of it. Walking away from a man who had shown her only kindness and love, whose baby she might be carrying, to go back to a man who treated her poorly. And if Anthony had reacted differently, I thought, perhaps this whole scene would have been changed. Perhaps they would be planning the start of their family, even now.

Becca wasn't quite herself for the rest of the day; she couldn't settle to anything. Each time she sat down on the floor to play with Samuel, she lost concentration after a couple of minutes and ended up staring out of the window. When Ryan came home, the sound of the door made her jump. Usually, she'd started on dinner before he arrived.

'Hey,' Ryan said, putting his head around the door of the living room. 'I'm going for a shower. What's for dinner?'

'Hi,' Becca said. 'I'm not sure yet. I'll have a look at what we've got in the fridge.'

Ryan looked surprised but said nothing, and a few seconds later, we heard the sound of the shower starting up.

It bothered me that he never made a point of coming in and seeing Samuel at the end of his working day. I often wondered whether it bothered Becca. It must have done. After his shower, he usually came in and picked Samuel up. Perhaps it was that. That he just wanted to freshen up first. But I knew from the times Becca had been away from Samuel for a few hours that she couldn't wait to see him. That she wouldn't let anything get in the way of that first cuddle.

Becca left Samuel looking at a board book and opened the fridge. There were eggs and a bag of carrots, a couple of beers, some butter, milk, cheese. She would make omelettes, I thought. She'd boil carrots to go with them and if there was a bag of chips in the freezer, she'd put those in the oven. As I thought it, she opened the freezer and began to rummage through the drawers.

Half an hour later, they were sitting down at the table,

Becca spooning the contents of a jar of baby food into Samuel in between mouthfuls of her own meal.

'How was your day?' she asked.

Ryan nodded. 'Not bad. There's this guy, he's been in three times looking at the same car. Taken it for a test drive, asked hundreds of questions about its history. He's tried to knock me down on price a few times. I went down by £250 but then stuck firm. I thought he was going to walk away. But then he shook my hand. The boss was really impressed.'

Becca smiled.

'What about you? Did you go into town?'

'Yes. I bought a few things for the new baby.'

This was true. Before meeting up with Anthony, she had gone into Tesco and picked up some muslins, a few vests. She wasn't showing yet, but Ryan glanced down at her belly at the mention of the baby. The scan was in a couple of weeks, and I knew from things that Becca had said that that would make it all feel real. Last time, she hadn't wanted to discuss names before that first scan.

Ryan's phone rang in his pocket and he pulled it out. 'Yeah, oh hi, Carl.'

Becca finished her own food and turned her chair sideways so she was facing Samuel's high chair. He hadn't eaten much and he was starting to wriggle and fuss. Becca made faces at him, and he laughed, and when he opened his mouth, she pushed another spoonful of the orange mixture into it. Samuel frowned, annoyed at being tricked like that, but he didn't spit it out.

'Oh yeah? This afternoon?'

If Becca wondered what this conversation was about, she didn't show it. There were great pauses between Ryan's words, and his voice had taken on a bit of an edge. But he was like that, sometimes; quick to anger. I don't think Becca was worried at that point.

'Well, thanks for letting me know. You're a good mate. Yeah, we'll catch up soon, have some beers.'

He put the phone back in his pocket and said nothing. Becca went on feeding Samuel.

'How's Carl?' she asked.

'Fine,' Ryan said. 'Shouldn't you be putting the little guy to bed by now?'

He was right. It was seven o'clock, and Samuel was usually well on his way to being asleep by then. It was another sign that Becca wasn't really with it. She wiped his mouth and took him into the bedroom.

'No bath tonight, Sam-Sam. Mummy lost track of time.'

I desperately wanted to stay in the living room and keep an eye on Ryan. I thought I'd heard something straining in his voice after he ended his phone call, and I was worried. But wherever Becca went, I went too. So I hovered in the corner of the bedroom, nervously, while Becca got Samuel ready for bed, brushing his tiny teeth and changing him into a sleepsuit. She hummed a little, as she often did, and Samuel was calm and happy. Within ten minutes, he was lying in his cot, eyelids drooping, and Becca was creeping out of the room.

She jumped when she saw Ryan standing in the living room doorway, waiting for her.

'Tell me more about what you did this afternoon,' he said.

Becca walked over to the kitchen area, flicked on the kettle, and frowned. 'I went into town,' she said. 'Dad had Sammy for me. I bought a few things for the new baby and then went for a coffee.'

'Did you see anyone?' Ryan asked.

And I knew that she heard it then, that edge, because she

froze. She reached up to take the mugs from the cupboard before speaking again.

'I saw Anthony.'

'Anthony. The guy you were seeing when you moved out?'

He knows, I thought. Why does he have to torment her like this, drag the thing out?

'Yes,' Becca said, her voice small.

'And why didn't you mention that before?'

'I don't know. I guess I knew you wouldn't like it.'

'You're right, I don't. What else do you not tell me because you think I won't like it?'

'Nothing.'

'I don't believe you.'

They were standing very close together, and Becca took a couple of steps backwards, but Ryan caught her by the wrist.

'Carl saw you. He went past that fancy café near Boots and said he saw you with someone else, looking pretty cosy.'

Becca took a deep breath. 'We were just talking,' she said. 'I didn't arrange to meet him. He just came in and saw us and he asked how things were going.'

I wondered whether she would regret this lie. I didn't know how much Ryan knew, how much he could find out. If he knew that she'd lied about this, he might think she was lying about other things.

'And what did you tell him?'

'I said that things were good.'

Ryan nodded, but his face was set in an angry grimace. He's decided, I thought. It doesn't really matter what she says or does now. He's decided that she's betrayed him. And then his face changed slightly, and I realised that he was doing the maths.

'Hold on,' he said.

I looked at Lucy and it was clear in her face, and in Becca's, that we all knew what was coming.

'Could this baby you're carrying be his, Becca?'

'No!'

It was too much, too forceful, too sure.

'Did you come back here, knowing you were pregnant and that he wouldn't want to know? Did you come back here because you knew I would keep a roof over your head?'

'No.'

It was the truth, and yet Becca's voice cracked a little because there was a grain of a lie in it. She hadn't known she was pregnant when she came back, after all, but she had stayed once she found out, knowing that the baby might not be Ryan's. And Ryan heard her falter, and he pounced on it.

'You're lying!' He pulled on Becca's wrist until she jerked towards him awkwardly.

'No, I...' Becca stopped, looked down at her wrist, which Ryan was still gripping tightly. 'You're hurting me!'

'Then tell me the truth. It's very simple. Are you still sleeping with him? Are you making me look like an idiot while I work all hours to look after you and your babies?'

Your babies. Those words stung her, I could tell. And they hung in the space between them, refusing to disappear.

'No, Ryan! I ran into him, and he wanted to know how we were. That's all, I swear.'

'Is he trying to get you back? Is that it?'

'No, he's going away, isn't he? He's just home for the summer and then he's going back to uni. I'll probably never see him again!'

I snuck a look in Lucy's direction at that, and she looked horrified. If Becca was right, and nothing more would ever happen between her and Anthony, there would be no Lucy. But of course, no one could know, could they? It wasn't that she might be lying, rather that she might be wrong. It was the future, and how could anyone know?

'I don't think I believe you,' Ryan said.

And then he shoved her away from him, hard, and everything seemed to slow down, and her body seemed tiny as it moved through the cramped space of the flat. They'd been standing close to the kitchen worktop, the mugs Becca had got out of the cupboard for a cup of tea forgotten, and I saw before it happened that she was going to fall against the corner of the counter. I looked to Lucy as if I thought she could somehow stop it. And her look was full of horror, but also a warning. Her look said: *See, is this what you want for her?*

Becca collapsed against the kitchen worktop and put her hands protectively to her stomach, but it was too late. She'd knocked against the counter hard; it had winded her. I looked back and forth between her and Ryan, saw him realise what he'd done. He covered the space between them and reached for her.

'Shit, are you okay?'

Becca couldn't meet his eye at first. Or wouldn't.

'I need to go to the hospital,' she said, her voice the coldest I'd ever heard it. 'It hurts. I need them to check on the baby.'

I expected Ryan to bluster, to say she was overreacting, to try to calm her down. But he must have heard that shift in her voice, too, because he simply said, 'I'll get Sammy.' I watched Becca's face; she was conflicted. Samuel was fast asleep and I understood that she didn't want him woken and carried around, spending hours in an A&E waiting room. But she couldn't drive.

'Leave him,' she said at last. 'I'll call my dad. Get him to take me.'

'Okay, if that's what you want. Fuck, I can't believe this. I was angry and I just wasn't thinking. I didn't mean—'

'I know,' Becca said. And it was clear from her voice that she didn't want him to say anything else. Although perhaps an apology might have been welcomed. But none was forthcoming.

19

JULY 2023

Becca sat in the waiting room with her dad beside her, Lucy and I waiting in the shadows. Every now and again, she clutched at her stomach and her dad reached out and squeezed her hand. It was strange, I thought, how it was a little like a scene of someone in labour. And yet, it might be the opposite. It might be the end.

'What are you thinking?' I asked Lucy. We'd been waiting for twenty minutes, but it felt more like a couple of hours. I couldn't understand why they weren't calling her through, why she wasn't top priority. But then, there were so many people in that space who were in pain. They couldn't prioritise her just because we loved her so much. I looked around the room. Some of the women had Almosts with them, and they all looked worried, like us. None of them would meet my eye.

'I don't know, Eliza,' Lucy said. 'I'm trying not to think anything, until we hear some news.'

Samuel and I had always been so close, when the four of us were together, and I knew it had been the same for Lucy and Thomas. Did she love him just the way I'd loved Samuel? I think she did. I tried to put myself in Lucy's position, to imagine how I would feel if this were Samuel whose life was on the line. It was bad enough that it was Thomas, but thinking of it being Samuel was physically painful, like a small ball of fire inside me, growing.

'I'm sorry,' I said.

'What do you have to be sorry for? You didn't cause it.'

'I'm just sorry.'

When Becca was five, she fell off her bike while learning to ride it and cut both of her knees pretty badly. She was sitting on the pavement, crying, and her dad was beside her, his arm around her and her bike behind him. I remember him saying sorry, and her asking, through tears, why he was saying that when it wasn't his fault. I remember him telling her that you could be sorry about something that wasn't your fault. That you could just be sorry that it happened. And that was the kind of sorry I was, then. Sorry for Lucy, whose heart was breaking. And Becca, who didn't deserve this. And me, because I was hurting too. I was sorry for all of us.

When they said Becca's name, she jerked slightly, and I realised she'd fallen asleep, her head on her dad's shoulder. She'd had to tell him, in the car, about the pregnancy. And I'd thought what an awful thing that was, that she was breaking the news like this, on the way to the hospital, rather than with smiles and laughter and a scan photo to share. He hadn't asked many questions about what had happened that night and how, but I thought probably the doctors and nurses would. What would she say?

'Do you want me to come in with you, or wait here?' her dad asked.

'Come with me,' Becca said.

She was a little girl again. Of course, she wasn't much more than a little girl anyway, but I forgot that when she was with Samuel, when she was functioning as a mother. But something about her being hurt, and being back with her dad, made all that fall away and I saw a lost, scared girl. She stood and went towards the man who had called her name, and her dad followed behind, his hands out in front of him, as if ready to catch her if she fell.

They were led into a small, stuffy room. There was a fan blowing warmish air around.

'Rebecca Valentine?' the man asked, and Becca nodded.

'I'm a duty nurse. Can you tell me what happened?'

'I fell against the kitchen counter,' she said, her voice barely more than a whisper.

'How did you fall? Were you dizzy? Did you lose consciousness at all?'

'No, nothing like that. I was arguing with my boyfriend and he sort of pushed me away from him and I fell.'

Her dad's face was pure anger. He'd probably suspected that there was more to this than an innocent trip, but it was different having it explained in front of him.

'So more of a push than a fall, then?' the nurse asked kindly.

'He didn't mean to do it. He was just worked up and he gave me a little push and somehow I fell and—'

'Love,' her dad cut in, 'don't feel you have to defend him. You're pregnant with his baby and he pushed you. That's pretty unforgiveable in my book.'

Becca said nothing, looked down. Her hair made curtains at either side of her face and it was impossible to see her expression.

The nurse looked from Becca to her dad and then spoke

again. 'Right, I was just about to come on to the pregnancy. How many weeks?'

'Ten. We've got a scan booked in a couple of weeks.'

I thought about how that visit to the same hospital might be, if things were fine. How Ryan would be jovial, tucking his hand into the back pocket of Becca's jeans. How the sonographer would say everything was looking good, that the baby was developing well but it was a bit too early to determine the sex. How Lucy and I would share a look, wishing we could tell them that it was a boy, that it was Thomas. I could see that scene so clearly, and yet it might not come to pass.

'Are you in pain?' the nurse asked.

'Yes,' Becca said. 'It comes and goes. Waves. I've taken a couple of paracetamol, while we were waiting.'

'Right, I think we'd better do a scan to see what's going on,' the nurse said. 'I'll arrange that. You go back to the waiting room, and try not to worry. We'll call you back through as soon as we can.'

Becca and her dad walked back to the seats they'd been occupying before in silence.

'Do you want a tea or anything?' he asked.

'Can you get me some chocolate?'

He nodded and disappeared to the vending machines, feeling in his pocket for change. When he came back, he handed Becca a Dairy Milk and blew on his small, steaming plastic cup.

'How long has this been going on?' he asked. It was clear to me that it had taken a lot for him to ask, that he'd chosen his words carefully. He'd probably tested them out while he waited for the hot drink.

'It's not like that,' Becca said. 'It's not something that's going on. It's something that happened, once, tonight, and he didn't mean it. It was an accident.'

'I don't like you covering for him like that. If he pushed you—'

'It was barely a push!'

'Regardless,' her dad went on, 'if he pushed you, that's not okay. And it was hard enough for you to fall onto the kitchen worktop, so it wasn't nothing, love. What are things like between you day to day?'

'They're good,' Becca said.

I thought about the day to day. About the way they laughed together, sometimes, when they were eating dinner and the way he put his arm around her when they were sitting on the sofa in the evening. There was that, but there was also the way he left things to her, not really pulling his weight when it came to cleaning or cooking or looking after their son. The way he made her feel like she was being unfair if she didn't want to have sex. The way he did other things when she was talking, as if he didn't care enough to listen.

But it was all she knew, I thought. Becca's parents hadn't exactly given her an example of a loving relationship to aspire to, and she'd moved in with Ryan when she was so young. She didn't know what was normal and what she could expect.

'You know,' her dad said, his voice softer, 'you can always come back to me. You and Sammy and this little one. Don't ever feel like you don't have anywhere to go.'

Becca looked as though she might cry, and she gave a nod, and then her name was called, and they were on their way to the scan that would determine her future. Or some of it, at least.

It must have been bittersweet for Becca, climbing up onto that bed in that room two weeks before her scan was due. Her dad beside her instead of her boyfriend. Her boyfriend at home looking after their son, while she waited to hear the fate of her second child. The sonographer frowned as he spread the jelly on Becca's tummy and frowned as he peered at the screen. I told myself that the frowning meant nothing, that he couldn't possibly know. Not yet.

But a couple of minutes later, he did.

'I'm sorry,' he said. 'There's no heartbeat here.'

Becca's dad was already holding her hand but he gripped it more tightly, turned his face away a little. And Becca turned onto her side and curled into a ball, and neither of them said anything.

'I'm sorry,' the sonographer said again. 'I'll give you a few minutes to get dressed, and then I can talk you through what to expect over the next couple of days.' He handed her a big wad of tissue paper to wipe up the jelly, and left the room.

The silence grew heavy. Becca didn't move. She was mourning a child she would never know. A child, a boy, who she would have named Thomas. I could feel Lucy watching me and I met her gaze. There was so much pain in her eyes that I didn't know what to do to take some of it away.

'I hate him,' Lucy said. 'I'll always hate him, no matter what.'

And did I hate him? My father, my father-to-be? I didn't. I couldn't. I knew he'd done this, and that there were parts of him that were so bad they were rotten, but I couldn't hate him. Not quite.

'Come on, love,' her dad said, his voice thick. 'Let's get you dressed.'

And as if she were a child, he turned her onto her back and used the tissue to wipe her belly, pulled down her top, and then lifted her off the bed and onto the floor. I didn't think she'd take her own weight, but she did. She looked up at her dad and there was nothing in her eyes. It was more terrifying than the hatred I'd seen in Lucy's. Just blankness. Just absence.

There was a soft knock at the door and the sonographer returned. He told Becca she would probably bleed on and off for a few days, that the foetus would make its way out like that. In a week, she would come in for another scan, and they would check that it was all gone. If it wasn't, they would perform a small procedure to fix that.

It was a lot to take in. Her dad nodded and I knew he was trying to remember it all so he could fill Becca in later, when she was ready to hear it. Once it was over, he stood and Becca followed suit, and they walked out of the hospital without a word. He paid for the parking, Becca kicked at stones with the toes of her trainers, and then they got in the car, and it seemed like it had been years since they'd last been in it, since they'd driven to the hospital, still hoping.

'I don't want to take you back there,' her dad said when they were a few miles from home. 'I'm worried for you.'

'I have to go back,' Becca said, her voice low. 'Sammy's there. I need to look after him.'

'You need to be looked after, love. You've got a tough few days ahead. Maybe I could take Sammy for you?'

'No,' Becca said. 'I need him with me.'

I could see it from both sides. Her dad wanted to protect her, wanted to make it as easy for her as he could, but Becca had just lost a child and she couldn't face losing her remaining one, not even temporarily. Samuel was the one who would get her through this. But that still left the question of Ryan. Would she forgive him for what he'd done? Would she stay?

'Take me home,' Becca said after a long beat of silence. 'I'm really tired. I just want to get some sleep.'

It was almost midnight. The night sky was coal-black. There were no stars visible.

'Have you told Ryan the news?' her dad asked.

'No. I didn't want to tell him over the phone.'

Her dad said nothing, but it was clear what he thought. That Ryan did not deserve this compassion, when he had been the one to cause this. The car was full of his resentment and anger, and her sadness.

When they got to the flat, her dad turned off the engine.

'Are you sure?' he asked. 'It's not too late. It's never too late to change your mind. I want you to know that. You never have to stick with something just because you decided it.'

'I'm sure,' Becca said. She unclipped her seatbelt and opened the car door.

I wanted her to say thank you to her dad, for being there, for doing everything right. I knew that she would have, ordinarily. But not that night. She was too heavy, too sad. She just got out of the car and made her way to the door. Her dad opened his window an inch or two.

'Becca?' he said.

She turned back.

'Goodnight. I love you.'

Becca said nothing, but she pressed a hand to her heart. And then she turned and went inside, and I wished I didn't have to go with her, that there was another way. Because it was clear to me that nothing good was going to happen inside that flat that night.

20

JULY–OCTOBER 2023

Becca let herself into the flat and went to the living room, but it was in darkness. She went to the bedroom next. Ryan and Samuel were curled up in bed together, both fast asleep. She watched them for a minute or two, and then she got undressed and slipped into the bed beside them.

'She should wake him and tell him what he's done,' Lucy said.

I'd been thinking the same thing. Actually, I'd been thinking that I couldn't believe he could fall asleep, not knowing.

But she didn't wake him. She didn't fall asleep herself, though, not for another two hours or more. She turned on her side, on her back. She got out of bed and went to the toilet, saw that the blood was starting to come, and put a thick sanitary towel in her pants. She stood in the dark kitchen and drank a glass of water. She watched her sleeping boyfriend and son. She waited for sleep to come.

Samuel woke before six, as he always did, and Ryan tried to shush him, but he was wide awake. Becca looked exhausted, but she picked Samuel up anyway and took him over to the mat they kept on the floor for changing his nappy.

'I didn't hear you come in,' Ryan said. 'Is everything okay?'

'No,' Becca said.

She blew a raspberry on Samuel's tummy and he giggled and kicked his legs, and then she pulled off the full nappy and put it in a bag, took a wipe from the packet. These were the things she did now, all the time. She could perform them without thinking.

'What do you mean? Is the baby...?' Ryan asked.

'There's no baby. No heartbeat.'

I listened for the crack in Becca's voice but didn't hear it. She sounded stronger than she had the night before.

Ryan got out of bed and kneeled down on the floor beside Becca. 'Babe,' he said. He put his arm around her but she shrugged it off. 'You know, we can have another baby...'

I couldn't help but feel excited. If they had another baby, that would be me. I felt Lucy looking at me but kept my gaze down, kept my giddiness inside. It wasn't appropriate, when we were mourning Thomas. And it was too soon, anyway. There was still over a year to go before my conception date.

'It doesn't work like that,' Becca said. She'd finished doing up Samuel's poppers and she lifted him up to standing, let him toddle off. He'd been walking for a couple of weeks and I loved to watch him, the way he tried, the way he fell. 'You can't just replace your dead baby with another one. It hasn't even come out of my body yet. Jesus.'

'It's a shock,' Ryan said, 'I understand that. But in time, you'll feel better and then we can try again. It's not like you've struggled to get pregnant in the past.'

He'd tried for a joke but it fell flat.

'Do you want a cup of tea?' he asked.

It was such a normal question, but it stood out because Ryan rarely asked it. It was always her doing things for him, I realised. For both him and Samuel. It was always her giving, him taking.

'Yes, please,' she said.

Neither of them made any reference to his part in what had happened. She didn't say out loud that it was his fault. But it was there, in the air. Waiting.

* * *

Later, Lucy came to me.

'Where do you think he is?' she asked.

'Thomas?' I knew she meant Thomas. I was stalling for time. I didn't know the answer. Couldn't know.

Lucy nodded. 'Because if he's somewhere else, some other world like this one, then maybe I don't want to be born at all. Maybe I want to go there, to be with him.'

I hadn't expected this.

'I don't know, Lucy,' I said. 'I just don't know. They don't know about us, being here, so there could be any number of other worlds and states, couldn't there? I don't know how we'd find out.'

'No,' Lucy said. 'I don't know either.'

And she was silent after that. But I felt her presence beside me, all day.

* * *

Becca's dad kept a close eye on things after that night. He came round more often, invited Becca to come to the house. He asked her questions. Was she okay? Was Ryan treating her well? Was she safe? It was clear that she resented having to answer them, but I knew that she could see, too, that they came from a good place. From a place of loving her and wanting to protect her. So she never snapped or told him not to ask them. She just answered them the same way every time. *Yes, I'm okay. Yes, Ryan's looking after me. Yes, I'm safe. Of course I'm safe. Do you think I would stay somewhere if I wasn't?*

Her dad never answered that one. He just tilted his head to one side and looked at her with such sadness that I could barely stand it. His look said that he'd wanted more for her, and I thought of the nights he'd spent rocking her to sleep when she was a baby. How could he have known, back then, that they would be here? Him living alone in their family house, and her a mother so young and living with a man who might have caused her miscarriage. It was too much.

She started to go home most Saturday nights. Ryan often went out for drinks with Carl, and Becca's dad would come to the flat and pick up Becca and Samuel, take them back to the house. Sometimes, they'd stay overnight. Now that Samuel was a bit older, he didn't need as much stuff. It was easier for them to go places. So they went to her dad's and ate a meal together, and then her dad would put Samuel down to sleep while Becca had a long soak in the bath, and afterwards, she would sit on the sofa with her dressing gown on and her hair wet, and they would watch a film. In the morning he would make pancakes and they would sit around the table and I would see that this was what a family should be like.

'She needs to leave him,' Lucy said, every single time.

'Maybe she will,' I said.

I tried to keep the fear out of my voice. We both knew what leaving Ryan meant for me.

* * *

Whenever I could, I tried to communicate with Samuel. I couldn't believe that the connection we'd had, when we were together, had come to nothing. I felt sure it must mean something. I felt sure that if I tried hard enough, or worked out the right way, I would be able to break through the membrane that separated us and make him feel me. Whenever we were in the same room, I began to lie or sit or stand right beside him. I curled around him in his cot, I sat beside him on the playmat, I walked the path from living room to kitchen to bedroom with him, over and over. Did it make any difference? Did he know I was there? I don't know. I liked to think so. Sometimes, he would turn his head a little and we'd be mere inches apart, and I would stare at him, and he would put out a tentative finger or seem to search with his eyes, and I would be sure he was aware of me. But other times, he did none of those things, and I felt it was all for nothing.

'What are you doing?' Lucy asked.

'I'm trying to get him to know that I'm there.'

'But don't you think, if that were possible, that people would have done it before us?'

I'd thought about that. But there must be a first time for everything, mustn't there? And if no one ever tried, nothing new would ever be achieved.

'Maybe no one has ever tried hard enough,' I said.

Lucy didn't answer, but I knew she thought it was hopeless. I wanted her to ask me what I would do if I could get through to him; what I would say or ask or suggest. Because I wanted to know the answer to that myself. But I pushed that reservation away whenever it came too close and focused hard on the task of getting him to notice me. What else did I have to do, after all?

* * *

In October, three months after Becca lost Thomas, it seemed like she was the only one who thought about him. And Lucy and me, of course. More Lucy than me. I missed him, of course I did, but it was nothing like the ache I'd felt when Samuel was conceived. And then, there had been the hope that we'd see him again, that we'd get to watch over him. Whereas Thomas was gone, and we had to learn to accept that.

Things between Becca and Ryan had been strained. He'd never said sorry, never admitted that it had been his fault. She had never accused him outright. But they'd been living beside one another, rather than together. Eating meals at different times, going to bed separately, sitting at either end of the sofa in the evening and watching rubbish on TV. It was worse, in a way, than slammed doors and shouting. It was like a slow, quiet death.

One evening, much like any other, they were on the sofa. The TV was on and showing a documentary about a serial killer in the USA, and neither of them were really watching it. Samuel was asleep; had been for a good couple of hours. And then something happened that hadn't happened for a long time. Ryan reached across the space between them and covered Becca's hand with his. She didn't acknowledge it at first, but there was a miniscule change to the expression on her face. It wasn't a smile, nothing as straightforward as that. It was a lightening, I suppose. A cloud slowly lifting.

'Becca,' he said, and she turned her face towards him. 'Are we okay?'

'I don't know,' she said. 'I mean, we haven't been, have we? But I'm hoping we can be again.'

He shuffled towards her, put his arm around her shoulders.

And when she turned towards him again, he kissed her. It was gentler than his usual kisses. It didn't ask anything of her. It didn't seem like a precursor to sex. When it ended, I saw that there were tears on Becca's face.

'I can't stop thinking about the baby,' she said. 'I would have been almost six months by now. We would have known the sex and been choosing names. I would have been starting to get backache and finding it difficult to sleep. When I'm here on my own with Sammy, I think about how hard it would be, having two of them, and how Sammy might feel left out and like he'd been replaced. But then I think about how it feels to hold a brand-new baby in your arms and fall asleep lying next to it, and I get so upset. I just wish we'd been given a chance, you know? I feel like we deserved a chance.'

It was the most she'd spoken for weeks on end and Ryan seemed a little stunned by it.

'Is it the same for you?' she asked.

'No,' Ryan said, and Becca looked at him quizzically, hurt gathering in her eyes.

Ryan cleared his throat a little self-consciously and took his arm from around Becca's shoulders to rub his eyes. Was he crying? I'd never seen him cry.

'No, it's not the same for me. I think it will always be harder for the mum. My life hasn't changed too much. We were having a baby, and then we weren't. I was sad, of course I was. But I believe we'll have another one, in the future. I can move on from it. But I can understand how different it would be if that baby had been growing in my body.'

Becca didn't say anything, and I wondered whether she was rolling that 'was' around her mind, the way I was. *Was* sad. I *was* sad.

'Do you think you can get past it?' he asked. 'Because I think, if you can't, that it might be the end of us.'

Becca looked at him, alarmed. She hadn't been expecting that, I could see. It was true that they hadn't been living as a couple, not really, but was he really putting a time limit on her grief? It was too much and I wanted her to say so.

'I have to,' she said. 'I can't let it ruin my whole life.'

'No,' Ryan said. 'No, you can't let it do that.'

The TV had been on in the background throughout this exchange, and phrases kept breaking through. 'Cold-blooded', 'stalked his prey', 'never knew what a normal childhood was like'. I felt like, if I had a body, I would be shivering.

'For fuck's sake,' Lucy muttered. 'He's the one who's going to ruin her whole life.'

'Maybe they'll get over it, both of them, and then...'

'It sounds like he's pretty okay about it already, doesn't it? I don't understand how she seems to have forgiven him for what he did.'

'It was an accident,' I said, and then I stopped myself.

'It wasn't and you know it,' Lucy said, her voice sharp and cold as ice.

I tried to replay the events of that evening, painful as it was. I could see Ryan pushing her away, but it was gentle, his eyes were kind. Was I misremembering? Was I giving him too much credit? Lucy obviously thought so. I tried to think back to how I'd felt at the time, tried to see her fall, but it was too much, and I looked away.

Perhaps this was a part of it all, I thought. Perhaps you just couldn't think too badly of one of your own parents. It was okay for Lucy, knowing that her father was Anthony. She was free to hate Ryan and wish for the demise of their relationship, but what about me? If they ended, I would never begin. And it was built into me to fight for my existence.

* * *

That night, Ryan and Becca had sex for the first time since the miscarriage. It seemed like a way of coming back together, of comforting one another. After it, Ryan stayed awake for a long time, stroking Becca's hair rhythmically. Becca was the first to fall asleep, which was unusual. I wished I had access to his mind. I was always wishing that about Becca but this was the first time I'd wished it about him. But it was futile. I decided I'd be better off just focusing on the one thing I was hoping to be able to control. I slipped into the cot beside Samuel, and curled around his sleeping body.

21

APRIL 2024

When Becca saw Anthony again, all I felt was a cold, pure dread. After all, the last time this had happened, it had ended with Becca losing the baby. Losing Thomas. And while that clearly hadn't been Anthony's fault, one thing had, in some cruel and twisted way, led to the other.

I could see that Lucy's feelings about it were conflicted. It was more complicated for her than it was for me. Every meeting with Anthony gave her hope, but like me, she hated to see Becca hurt.

This time it was worse, more dangerous, because he came to the flat. One minute, Becca was playing on the floor with Samuel, and the next, the buzzer was going, and she'd scooped Samuel up and was heading down the hallway. When she opened the door and saw Anthony standing there, her mouth dropped open and she said nothing for long enough that it started to feel a bit awkward.

'Can I come in?' he asked.

'No,' Becca said, still flustered. 'I'll get our things and we'll go to the park.'

Anthony stood on the doorstep while Becca gathered up Samuel's water bottle and a snack and checked the bag for nappies and wipes. I felt like there was a higher chance of someone seeing him out there than if he came inside, but I understood, too, why she didn't let him in. There were boundaries that had to be maintained. If Ryan ever asked if Anthony had been inside this flat – and it was the kind of question he would ask, after all – Becca could say no with a clear conscience. And that was something.

They didn't say much on the short walk to the local park. Becca pushed the buggy and Anthony kept his hands in his pockets. Becca was the first to speak, just as they were rounding the corner at the top of her road.

'What are you doing here? What were you thinking? If Ryan had been here...'

She didn't need to finish that sentence. We all knew what would have happened if Ryan had opened that door.

'I just wanted to see you,' Anthony said. 'I heard from Ellie about what happened, about you losing the baby.'

Becca bit her bottom lip, hard, and I thought she was probably trying to keep herself from crying.

'The thing is, it sounded like it might not have been an accident,' Anthony went on, 'and I can't just let things go, knowing that. I need to know that you're okay. I accept that you've chosen to be with him, it's not about that. I just need to be absolutely sure that you are safe.'

'You sound like my dad,' Becca said, and there was a shadow of a smile on her face.

Anthony shrugged. They'd reached the park and he held open the gate while Becca pushed the buggy through. She reached in and unclipped the straps and lifted Samuel out, and he toddled off in the direction of the small climbing frame.

Becca looked around her, and I thought she was probably checking for faces she knew, but it was a drizzly day and the park was deserted. In one corner, a grandmother pushed a little girl on a swing. Other than that, they had the place to themselves. They followed Samuel and helped him as they talked, Anthony at one side of the bright-red climbing structure and Becca at the other. A team. The first time he reached the little slide and hurtled down it, his face was pure joy and Anthony laughed out loud.

'He's brilliant,' Anthony said.

'Isn't he?' Becca replied.

And I wondered whether she was noticing, like I was noticing, that this was the kind of thing Ryan never did, never said. I couldn't remember the last time they'd gone to the park as a family.

'Becca, the baby you lost...'

'I can't talk about it,' Becca said.

Anthony nodded and hung his head.

'He knows,' Lucy said. 'He knows Thomas was his, and he knows what Ryan did. He's going to rescue her.'

'It's not a fairytale,' I said.

She didn't answer. We were snapping at one another more and more. It was inevitable, I suppose. While we were there, side by side, observing and never getting involved in the action, a battle of sorts was taking place between us. And only one of us could win.

'So what can we talk about?' Anthony asked, his voice low but steely. 'How he treats you? What happened the night you lost the baby?'

Becca plastered a smile on her face for Samuel, who was just coming down the slide for about the twentieth time, and then she turned to Anthony, her expression a mixture of anger and fear.

'It was an accident,' she said.

'What? What was? Pretend I know nothing about it and tell me what happened. Because when I saw you in the café, you were looking forward to your scan and everything looked good. And the next thing I know...'

'Okay, so Ryan was angry about me running into you and he pushed me away from him, but it wasn't hard, and it didn't hurt. It wasn't his fault that I fell onto the corner of the kitchen worktop. It was just one of those things.'

'How can you say that? One of those things? I have never once pushed someone so hard they fell. It's not okay for him to treat you like that.'

'It is if I let him,' Becca said. She said it so quietly that I almost missed it, and Anthony did.

'What was that?' he asked, leaning closer, holding Samuel's hand as he made his way across a wobbly wooden bridge.

'I said it's my decision,' Becca hissed. 'I love him.'

'Tell me why,' Anthony said. 'Tell me what you love about him.'

'I don't have to do that. You said it wasn't about that. And now you just sound jealous. The time we spent together, I've put it behind me. I just wish you could do the same.'

Anthony crouched down to Samuel, who'd just managed the steps up to the slide for the first time without assistance, and gave him a high-five.

'Do you want me to go? It's just, you don't seem very happy in this life you've made.'

'You're wrong,' Becca said. 'I'm happy.'

'Okay. Well, then, I'll leave you to it.'

Becca stood very still as Anthony brushed a hand through

Samuel's hair and said he'd see him later. She stood still as he walked away. And when he was at the gate, he turned, as I think we'd all known he would.

'I'm home for Easter for a few weeks,' he said. 'If you change your mind about anything.'

'Goodbye,' Becca said, and if you didn't know her really well, you might have missed the slight quake to her voice.

Anthony nodded, once, then turned and walked away.

* * *

That evening, I felt like I was holding my breath. Waiting for Ryan to reveal that he knew Becca had been with Anthony that day. When Samuel was in bed and they were sitting on the sofa eating the pasta Becca had made, Ryan said there was something he wanted to talk about, and I felt like I was frozen, waiting.

'What?' Becca asked.

And I could see that she was scared, too. What would he do to her this time?

'I think we should have another baby,' he said.

Becca let out a breath in a rush and laughed a strange sort of laugh that I hadn't heard from her before.

'What's so funny?' Ryan asked. 'We were going to have two, weren't we? And I'd got used to the idea. I just wondered whether you felt like you were ready to try again.'

Months had passed since the miscarriage. Not far off a year. At the hospital, they'd told Becca that she should wait at least three months before trying again. And she had said there was no chance of another baby for a good while. I'd wondered, at the time, whether she'd meant because she wasn't going to be with Ryan any more. She still hadn't said anything, but she was looking at Ryan with a curious expression.

'Well?' he asked.

'I'm thinking,' she said.

'Okay, well don't think too long or I might change my mind.'

Ryan put his empty bowl down on the floor and pulled Becca close to him.

'Oy,' she said. 'Still eating here.'

He let her go, but not before he'd planted a kiss on her temple.

'What was that for?' she asked.

'For thinking about it,' he said, his voice thick.

He was thanking her, I thought, for staying with him after what he'd done. It was an admission of sorts. Not an apology, but something. Something I couldn't have imagined him doing six months earlier. He was changing, I thought. Growing up. And perhaps it wasn't too late for them to have a healthy, loving relationship. Another child. Me.

'I know what you're thinking, Eliza,' Lucy said, an edge of humour in her voice.

'No, you don't.'

'I do. You're thinking he's softening up, growing as a person, becoming the kind of partner she really needs.'

I said nothing. What was there to say?

'He hasn't changed,' she said. 'I don't know what this is, but it won't last.'

* * *

And she was right. It didn't. A few days later, a Saturday, Ryan went out for drinks with Carl and came back drunk and itching for a fight. Becca was asleep, but he made so much noise clattering about that she woke up. Samuel, too.

'What are you doing?' Becca hissed, throwing off the covers and going over to Samuel's bed.

'For fuck's sake, I'm just getting ready for bed.'

Samuel was sitting up, his face collapsed. There were no tears, but he was wailing. Now that he was a pretty reliable sleeper, he hated to be woken up. Becca picked him up and shushed him, patting his nappy-clad bottom and rocking on the balls of her feet.

'He's going to start copying everything we say soon, you know,' she said. 'I really don't want him to be swearing at the playground. Can you watch what you say around him?'

Ryan came up behind her and I imagined the feel of his breath on her neck. I imagined it was sour and hot.

'I'll talk however the fuck I like in this flat. I'm sick to death of being told what to do.'

Samuel had been calming, but something changed at that moment and the wails started up again, louder than ever.

'Jesus Christ!' Ryan shouted. 'What the hell is wrong with him?'

Becca turned to face him and there was panic in her eyes. But something else, too. Anger, red-hot and pure. Samuel was her first priority. She was a mother protecting her cub.

'There's nothing wrong with him! He was asleep, and he hates being woken up for no reason. So do I, for that matter.'

Ryan stormed off into the bathroom and slammed the door, and Becca got into bed with Samuel and tried to settle him down, but he was agitated, restless. When Ryan reappeared, she was still patting and trying to calm him.

'He's not sleeping in our bed,' Ryan said, getting in. 'He's too big. None of us will get any sleep.'

Becca sat up, Samuel still in her arms. 'He and I were sleeping perfectly well until you came home and started making all this noise. You're the only one who is causing a problem here. If you're not happy with the three of us in this bed, you can go and sleep on the sofa.'

Ryan looked surprised. I was scared, for a moment, that he might hit her. But instead, he did what she asked. He grabbed a pillow and left the room without looking back. It was the first time she'd really stood up to him. And that's what everyone says you need to do with bullies, isn't it? I hoped she wouldn't pay for it in the morning. Soon after Ryan left the room, Samuel settled back into a deep sleep, but Becca lay awake for an hour or more, long after the sound of Ryan's snores started to drift through from the other room.

* * *

In the morning, Becca carried Samuel through to the living room a little while after he woke. Ryan was lying on the sofa, eyes open.

'Hungover?' she asked.

He nodded. 'I don't really remember what happened when I came in. Was I a twat?'

Becca smiled a little thinly. 'Kind of,' she said.

'I'm sorry.'

Becca put bread in the toaster and teabags in mugs. Samuel toddled around, trying to open drawers and cupboards that Becca had put safety locks on. He kept coming back to her legs, wrapping himself around her as she made breakfast.

When they were sitting at the table, buttered toast in front of them and steam rising from their mugs, Becca spoke again. 'I don't know how you can talk about having another one, when things are like this,' she said.

It sounded like something she'd practised, something she'd thought about a lot.

'What do you mean?'

'Last night, you woke us up and then got angry because Sammy was crying. And that's another thing. We're still in this one-bed flat, with Sammy sleeping in our room. Where do you think we're going to put another baby?'

Ryan rubbed at his eyes and then his forehead, as if he could push his hangover back inside. 'I can start looking for a bigger flat, if that's what you want. I thought you were happy here. You never said.'

'I'm fine here, but there's barely room for three of us, let alone four. I just don't think you've thought it through. You like the idea of another baby, but I'll be the one who has to deal with all the hard work of it.'

'Fine,' Ryan said, and he sounded like a sulky child. 'We won't have another one then. It was just an idea.'

'And I'm considering it, I really am. I just think there are things we need to sort out before we can do it. That's all. Don't be grumpy.'

Ryan stood up, a slice of toast in his hand. 'I'm not in the mood for this. I'm going back to bed.'

Becca watched him go, and I watched her. Was she thinking about the crumbs he was dropping on the floor and would leave all over the bedcovers, that she'd have to hoover up? Or about the fact that he'd chosen to go out and get drunk the night before and now she was going to have to look after Samuel on her own for half the day while he recovered? Or neither of those things? Perhaps she was just wondering how she'd ended up here, in this life, when it was so far from what she'd expected.

'Here you go, little man,' she said, tearing off a corner of buttered toast and handing it to Samuel, who grinned and bit into it. 'Looks like it's just you and me. Shall we go on an adventure?'

Half an hour later, she'd packed a bag and they were off to the leisure centre to swim. And when they came back, Samuel smelling of chlorine and ready for a nap, Ryan still hadn't surfaced.

22

JUNE 2024

Just when I'd stopped expecting it, my efforts to connect with Samuel began to pay off. It was a quiet day, just Becca and Samuel in the flat. He was toddling around, picking things up and moving them, while Becca did bits of cleaning and tidying. I was walking beside Samuel, as I often did, and then he stopped near the door that led out into the hallway, quite abruptly, and turned as if looking at me. He was holding his tatty toy dog in his hand, and he held it out as if handing it to me.

'Samuel?' I said, my voice shaky. Hardly daring to believe.

'Za,' he said. 'Za. Za.'

I could feel Lucy watching me.

'Did you see?' I asked, near hysterical. 'Did you hear?'

'It's just a sound,' she said, but she seemed unsure.

'It isn't. He's trying to say Eliza.'

He'd been talking for a while, but he still babbled a lot of nonsense as well as words. Surely this couldn't be a coincidence. No. I was more sure than I'd ever been about anything. After me trying for weeks, hovering around him for months, he knew I was there. He remembered. He was still standing there, holding out the toy, and I wished more than I'd ever wished anything that I could take it from him.

'What are you doing, little man?' Becca asked.

She'd left the dishes she was in the middle of washing and started to walk over to him, her hands dripping.

Go back, I thought. *Go back, go back, go back, go back.*

It was ages since I'd tried to make Becca do anything. I'd been concentrating on Samuel for such a long time. But sure enough, she stopped walking and stood still in the middle of the living room.

'Sammy?' she said.

He turned to her. 'Za.'

'Za? What does that mean, baby? Come here.'

Becca reached out her arms and Samuel walked into them, and she swung him up in the air and planted a kiss on his forehead. 'What's za?' she asked, and he giggled.

I was still standing where I'd been when Samuel had been beside me. I was frozen there. I didn't want the spell to break.

'Samuel!' I shouted it.

He turned his head in my direction. I looked at Lucy and she returned my gaze. There was no denying it.

'Samuel!'

Again, he looked.

'Come here, Samuel,' I said.

There was a beat of silence, and then he wriggled out of Becca's grasp and toddled over to where I was standing. I laughed out loud.

'Thank you!' I shrieked. 'Thank you, Samuel.'

It was like having him back. For almost two years now, we'd had him, but only to look at. And this, it was like a reunion of sorts. I felt like I was in between worlds. Not quite with Lucy, not quite with Samuel. And for a second, I thought again of Thomas. Wondered where he was. My guess was that he was nowhere. But it was hard to believe it, sometimes.

* * *

Later, Lucy brought it up. 'It's amazing,' she said. 'I mean, I thought you were mad. All that walking up and down, following him. All that lying curled around him in the cot. I thought you were crazy. But it's worked. It's amazing. The only thing is, I don't know what you're going to do with it?'

I looked at her. Was she scared that I was going to think up some way to ensure it was me and not her who would be born? Of course she was. We were both scared of that. Couldn't not be.

'I don't know,' I said. 'I haven't really got that far. I just wanted to see if it was possible first.'

'Do you think you could control him?' she asked, tilting her head in the direction of Ryan. He was home from work by then, and he and Becca were sitting on the sofa, the TV on.

'No,' I said. 'I don't think so. I mean, with her, and with Samuel, there's a connection, isn't there?'

'But he's your dad,' Lucy said.

It was true. There was no reason to think that the connection between me and Ryan was any less strong than the one between me and Becca, but it didn't feel like that, somehow. It had never crossed my mind to try to get him to do something.

'Try it,' Lucy said. 'What have you got to lose?'

I didn't say anything for a moment. Was it some kind of trick, or trap? Was she trying to get me to make a wrong move? We'd always been allies of a kind, but there was no getting around the fact that we were enemies now, whether we wanted to be or not. It was her or me. We couldn't both be winners here.

* * *

A couple of days later, Ryan was playing with Samuel on the floor. He was building a tower of cardboard blocks, then letting Samuel knock it down, over and over. Becca was making the lunch. Lucy wasn't around. I'd been waiting for a chance to test her theory without her watching me. I didn't want to fail in front of her. I tried to block everything out, to concentrate. I stared at Ryan, getting as close to him as I could.

Stand up, I thought. *Stand up, stand up, stand up, stand up.*

I kept repeating it, over and over. At one point, he shifted on his knees and I thought he was going to do it, but he settled back down again.

Stand up, stand up, stand up, stand up.

Nothing. I turned my attention to Samuel.

'Samuel,' I said, 'look at me. It's Eliza.'

He blinked, and I waited. And then he lifted his head and looked in my direction.

'Za,' he said. 'Za.'

'Have you heard him, Becca?' Ryan called over to the kitchen area. 'He keeps saying za. Any idea what he might be trying to say?'

'I've heard that too,' she called back. 'No idea.'

It felt conclusive. I had some control over Becca and Samuel, but nothing when it came to Ryan.

* * *

Becca and Ryan limped on. Every month or so, it seemed like it might all come crashing down around them, but they always seemed to manage to pull it back from the brink. It wasn't love, I was pretty sure of that. I wasn't sure what it was. Obligation? Weariness? Lack of imagination? I thought often about the little girl Becca had been, how I never would have guessed that she would end up in this life. And it made me wonder about Samuel's future, made me hope there was something more than this ahead of him.

By the time Samuel turned two, Lucy was frantic. Time was ticking. My conception date was three months away; hers was seven. Neither of us had used our Chances, and we hadn't discussed it, because it was getting close to the wire, and it was hard to talk to your sister about how you planned to sabotage her prospects of living. I'd been racking my brains to think of the best way I could make use of my Chance, and I'd come up with nothing. And all the time I was watching her, to see what she might do. We were both as desperate as each other.

They had another party to celebrate Samuel's second birthday. It was a lot like the last one. The same guests, more or less. Becca's mum had a new man, Kevin, and she brought him along and kept sneaking glances at her ex-husband to see whether he was bothered by it. He wasn't. There was no one new in his life, but he seemed content. He lived for Becca and Samuel. Spent all the time with them he could.

At one point, when Kevin was in the toilet or getting a drink, Becca's mum came over to her.

'Kevin's going to move in,' she said.

Becca nodded. 'That's nice.'

I waited for her to say something that a mother would say. To say that Becca and Samuel should come over sometime, that she missed them and she was sorry she hadn't been a big part of their lives lately. And then she did say something that a mother would say. But it was none of the things I'd expected.

'You're a good mum, Becca.'

Becca looked at Liz, her eyes wide, her lips slightly parted. She looked as if she was about to say something, but no words came.

'I should have told you a lot sooner. You have something I always lacked. You're doing a really good job.'

She walked away before Becca could acknowledge what she'd said. And soon after, she brought Kevin over and said that it was time for them to go. They didn't hug. It seemed entirely possible, to me, that they wouldn't see one another again until it was Samuel's third birthday. But it didn't matter, because Becca's mum had given her something that she'd really needed. And I knew that it would have the power to set her free.

'Two!' Becca's dad said, clutching Samuel's chubby thigh when Becca brought him over to see his granddad.

'Two!' Samuel replied.

He was starting to talk more and more. He was beginning to put two or three words together. 'Blue car.' 'I do it.' 'Love you.' He thought 'updown' was one word. And he still said 'za' pretty often, and no one but me and Lucy had any idea why.

'I've brought you a present, little man,' Becca's dad said, turning and picking up a big square box and holding it out to Samuel. From his pocket, he took a much smaller package and gave it to Becca.

Becca carefully lowered Samuel to the floor and he started to tear at the bright-yellow paper.

'What is it?' she asked her dad in a whisper.

'His is a little ride-on scooter,' he said, his eyes dancing. He was more excited than Samuel about the present. Once Samuel had got the paper off, her dad pulled the scooter out of the box and quickly assembled it.

'And you'll have to open yours.'

Becca tore off the paper. Inside, there were four small wooden blocks. And carved into them, there were words. On one, Samuel's full name, on the next, his date of birth, and on the third, the name of the hospital where he'd been born. The final block was covered with tiny stars.

'Thank you,' Becca said, brushing away a tear.

She bent down and tried to show the blocks to Samuel but he only had eyes for the scooter. She lifted him onto the seat and showed him how to put his hands on the handlebar, and within a couple of minutes he was pushing himself up and down the room, a huge smile on his face.

'He's such a happy little boy,' her dad said.

'He is,' Becca agreed. 'But...'

'But what?'

Becca looked around, checked that no one else was in earshot, and then said something that surprised us all. 'I think it's about time he had a brother or sister.'

Was it what Becca's mum had said that had swung it? There was no way of knowing, but I thought it might just be.

I didn't look at Lucy, couldn't. It had looked, once, like she had this all sewn up, but now, things had turned around and it was starting to look like I couldn't fail. Becca hadn't heard from Anthony since that day in the park, and we hadn't heard her mention his name to anyone, either. It was looking more and more like that chapter of her life was over. Which meant that mine might be close to starting.

* * *

A little later, when they'd all had cake and everyone had gone home and Becca was washing up while Ryan helped Samuel tidy away his new toys and books, she said it to him.

'Hey,' she said, pulling her hands out of the washing-up bowl. Ryan was walking past her, on his way to the hallway cupboard with the scooter.

'What?' he asked.

'I think we should have another baby,' she said.

Ryan's face broke into a smile. 'Yeah?' he asked.

He went towards her, put his hands on her waist. She lifted her own hands, still covered in bubbles, and put them on the back of his head.

'Yes,' she said. 'I'm ready.'

They kissed, and Ryan moved his hands from her waist to her bum, and Samuel came into the kitchen and stood there, looking up at them.

'Za,' he said. 'Za.'

And then Becca started laughing, and Samuel joined in, and Ryan moved away from Becca and picked Samuel up, swung him high in the air.

And they looked like a family. A family I wanted to join. A family I was going to join. And I thought, for a minute, that it was all going to be okay.

23

JULY 2024

There followed a period of 'trying'. It was strange, seeing them have sex and talk afterwards about whether that might have been the time, knowing they were too early. With Samuel, it had happened the first time, and with Thomas, as far as Ryan was concerned, it had happened as soon as they'd got back together. So they were both convinced that she'd be pregnant in no time. The first time she got her period, she cried in the toilet.

'I got my period,' she said to Ryan after she'd dried her eyes.

'Really? Well, don't worry, it'll happen next month.'

'What if it doesn't?' she asked.

'What do you mean? We'll just keep trying.'

'What if that baby we lost... what if that was it for us?'

She was standing in the living room doorway, and he came over to her, put his arms around her.

'It wasn't,' he said.

'You don't know that.'

'I know.'

I wondered how he could be confident about something so

random and changeable. Was it just arrogance? Or perhaps the confidence was faked, and he was just trying to reassure her, trying to lift her? At least he cares enough to do that, I thought.

Things with Lucy were tense. If it was a race, I was nearing the finish line and she was stuck back at the start. I kept wanting to ask her how she was planning to use her Chance, but there didn't seem to be a good way to bring it up. And then, out of nowhere, she just told me.

'I thought I should let you know,' she said. 'I've been trying to come up with a plan, for intervening. And I think I've got something.'

'Okay,' I said.

'I was thinking about inhabiting Anthony's body, making him come back here or send her a letter or something, but I'm scared to, because of what happened with Thomas…'

We were both silent while we thought about our brother, about how he so nearly got to live.

'So I think the next best thing is trying to come between Becca and Ryan. If they split up again, I'm fairly confident that she'd get in touch with Anthony. There's no one else. So I'm going to inhabit him, Ryan, and cause an argument.' She paused. 'I just thought you should know.'

I knew her well enough to know that that final comment was a demand of sorts. She expected the same honesty from me. I was grateful that she'd told me. She didn't have to, after all. She could have just gone ahead and done it.

'When will you do it?' I asked.

'Soon,' she said. 'Because if I want them to split up and her to reach out to Anthony and the two of them to be in a position to create a baby by the time my date comes around, I need to move pretty fast.'

'Thanks,' I said.

'For what? For trying to split up your mum and dad before you've had a chance to be conceived?'

I gave a half-laugh. It did seem like a strange thing to thank someone for, when she put it like that.

'For telling me,' I said. 'For letting me be prepared.'

'You know,' she said, 'you still have your Chance, too. Have you thought about how you'll use it?'

Her wording was comical. Had I thought about it? I'd barely thought about anything else, for months. For years.

'I still don't know,' I said.

It was the truth. I just didn't know. I would have to see how her intervention panned out first, wouldn't I?

'Okay,' she said. 'When you do, will you tell me?'

I owed her that, didn't I? She'd done it for me.

'Yes,' I said. 'I will.'

I still pondered on the fact that we'd never live side by side as sisters, after spending two decades here, waiting. It didn't seem right. But I was learning that there was so much that wasn't right, wasn't fair. This was nothing special, nothing so different.

* * *

When Lucy had said soon, I hadn't realised quite how soon she meant. The following day, a Sunday, Becca and Ryan and Samuel were all at home doing nothing much, and I noticed that Lucy had slipped away. And the next thing I knew, it was starting.

'You know,' Ryan said, pausing the game he was playing on

his Xbox, 'I still don't know whether that baby you lost was mine.'

Becca looked up at him, her mouth hanging open. She was changing Samuel's nappy, kneeling on the floor. 'Why would you bring that up?' she asked.

'Because it's been playing on my mind. We're living here, as a family, and we're trying for another baby. But I don't know whether you've been faithful to me.'

'Ryan, when I was with Anthony, we weren't together...'

Ryan stood up. 'What does that matter? Don't try to change the subject...'

'I'm not changing the subject! I'm saying that I was never unfaithful. We split up, I saw someone else for a while, and then we got back together.'

'Yes, and then you were pregnant. Almost immediately. And I didn't really give it a second thought because you got pregnant with Sammy the first time. But now, this time, it's taking longer, and it just makes me wonder.'

Becca fastened Samuel's new nappy in place, stood him up and pulled his trousers up, gave him a pat on the bum. 'Go play, baby boy,' she said.

He toddled out of the room, into the hallway.

'I hate arguing in front of him,' Becca said, standing. 'You know that. I don't understand where all this is coming from.'

'I've told you,' Ryan said. 'It's been playing on my mind.' His face was twisted in anger and I looked hard at him, trying to see any trace of Lucy inside. But it was no good. She wasn't visible. She was just pulling the strings.

Becca walked over so that she was standing a few inches from Ryan. 'If you really want to talk about that baby,' she said, 'let's talk about the night I lost it.'

He hadn't been expecting that, you could see. He took a

small step back but Becca stepped forward, and it was as if she was daring him to push her again, the way he had that night.

'That was an accident,' Ryan said quietly.

'Was it? Because no one else seems to think that. The nurse in the hospital didn't think that, and my dad didn't think that.'

'What the fuck did you tell them?' Ryan hissed.

'I told them that we argued and you pushed me and I fell because that's what happened.'

Just then, Samuel came back into the room. He was carrying the dog toy he slept with every night, which was already tatty and losing its fur. In the other hand, he had a book. He walked over to them and held it up.

'Just a minute,' Becca said to him, her voice calm and kind, the way it always was for him. 'Just give Mummy a minute.' And then she looked back up at Ryan. 'I'm not perfect,' she said, 'but neither are you. And I think you should remember that next time you want to bring something up.'

Their eyes locked and neither of them moved or spoke, and then Samuel tugged on Becca's sleeve and she lifted him up and carried him to the sofa.

'What have you got?' she asked. 'That book about pigs and ducks, again? Come on then.'

* * *

Without fuss, Lucy appeared at my side again. It had been a failure, a pretty spectacular one. I couldn't look at her. Didn't want her to see that I was pleased, that I felt I had the upper hand with her Chance used and mine still to come.

'That was a disaster,' she said quietly.

There was no denying it. 'I'm sorry,' I said.

I was sorry, not that it had failed but that she had spent her time thinking it up, had built up her hopes, and failed. She was mine, after all, and I loved her. She was... not quite my sister, but someone who might have been a sister in another world, if things had been different.

'I don't know what to do, Eliza,' she said.

I turned my head.

'About what?'

'I don't understand what it's all been for, this time, if we don't make it? What's the point of these long, waiting years?'

'I don't know,' I told her.

I'd wondered the same thing, of course. And we'd all discussed it, in the early years when it all seemed theoretical and so far in the future that it didn't affect us, not really. I remember Samuel saying he thought there was another world where failed Almosts ended up. And there might be, of course there might. We were proof that the world Becca inhabited wasn't all there was. Who was to say where things ended, how far the boundaries stretched? Like Lucy had once said, perhaps Thomas was somewhere else, waiting for us. And perhaps she would get to join him.

'Don't despair,' I said. 'It's not over yet.'

It struck me then, for the first time, that both of us might lose. Ever since she'd come clean about her date, I'd thought that only she or I could be born. But, of course, it was possible that neither of us would be. Maybe Samuel would be the only lucky one of the four of us. Maybe both of our dates would come and go.

'I feel like it is,' Lucy said. 'Who even knows where Anthony is? She seems determined to stay with Ryan, even though he treats her like shit sometimes. I'll never understand it. I think it's too late, for me.'

What could I say? It did look that way, didn't it? There was no arguing that.

'I'm sorry,' I said again.

'I know you are.'

We didn't say anything else that night. Just stayed side by side, close, like a team, like a united front. Like sisters.

24

JULY 2024

Another week went by and everything tipped and changed in the most unexpected of ways. It was a Saturday, and Becca and Samuel had been up for a good couple of hours when Ryan emerged from their bedroom. He'd been out with Carl the night before, had got in at two in the morning.

'I need a coffee,' he said.

Becca looked up. She and Samuel were drawing on a huge sheet of paper she'd torn off a roll and taped to the floor. Samuel had fat crayons and she had colouring pencils that she'd bought for when he was a bit older but quite enjoyed using herself.

'Do you want one?' Ryan asked.

'Yes, please.'

He rarely offered, but it wasn't enough, that morning, to make her forget the hours he'd spent in bed when he could have been with them. When he brought the drinks over, he put Becca's on the coffee table and sat on the sofa cradling his own.

'How's the little man?' he asked.

Becca tilted her head slightly to one side. 'He's okay. How was your night?'

'It was good. We ran into some guys we used to go to school with, and it turned into a bit of a session. And then we went for a curry after.'

'Good. Listen, I really fancy going for a swim this morning. Would that be okay?'

Ryan looked taken aback. I was surprised too. Becca was more used to going without the things she wanted and needed than asking for them. Ryan had so rarely looked after Samuel on his own. I noticed that she hadn't asked him if it was okay for him to look after Samuel. That was implied. And how could he say no, after all the freedom he took for himself? The nights out, the hungover mornings in bed.

'What time?' Ryan asked.

'I mean, anytime now really. As long as it's all right with you.'

'Sure,' he said.

He wasn't going to admit that he didn't feel confident looking after his own son for an hour or two, but I was pretty sure he didn't. Half of me thought Becca would back down, say it didn't matter after all, but she didn't. She disappeared to the bedroom, came back with her things in a bag.

'Thanks,' she said. 'I miss swimming, you know. I've been meaning to get back to it. He's had his breakfast and I've made him a sandwich for lunch. It's in the fridge. He'll probably have a banana with it, or a pear. And a cup of milk?'

Ryan smiled, and I could see that he was grateful she'd told him those things without him having to ask.

'Do you know where everything is?' she asked.

I would have bet that he didn't. He rarely changed nappies or clothes. But I also knew that he would pretend otherwise.

'We'll be fine, won't we, little man?' Ryan asked, lifting Samuel up from the floor and onto his lap. 'You go, swim.'

Becca picked up the mug of coffee he'd made her and drained it in three big gulps.

'Thanks,' she said, and then she kissed Samuel on the top of his head and walked out, with me and Lucy behind her.

Until she was sixteen, Becca had swum competitively, only stopping when the Covid pandemic had closed the pools. Lucy and I had spent half our lives sitting at the edges of swimming pools. But since Samuel, she'd only ever been swimming with him, and so it was strange to see her with her swimming cap and goggles on, diving in the way she used to and making her way up and down the pool, her face turned to the side to take a breath every three strokes, her arms quick and sure. She'd lost speed in the past few years. Of course she had. All that training and then nothing. But her technique was flawless. I remembered her coach, Jane, the pride in her eyes when Becca picked up trophies.

'What do you think is going on?' Lucy asked me. 'Why swimming? Why now?'

I wasn't sure. But I was pleased. 'Maybe she's realised she has to trust him to help her out more,' I said. 'Maybe she wants to get her old self back a bit.'

Those were my best guesses, but I was as surprised as Lucy was. Something had shifted, but I wasn't sure what.

After half an hour, Becca climbed out of the pool. She stood under the shower in the changing room for five long minutes, her eyes closed and a smile on her face. And looking at her made me want to smile, too. She was coming back. She was returning to herself.

When she got back to the flat, Becca let herself in and walked down the hallway. The door to the living room and kitchen was closed, and she reached for the handle and then dropped her hand. She'd heard something. We'd all heard it. It was Ryan's voice, full of bile. And then Samuel, wailing.

I could see how much Becca wanted to burst in and reach for her crying boy, but she held back. She wanted to know what she was dealing with.

'— Two years old now, you should be getting better at this!'

More tears from Samuel, a long, plaintive wail that seemed like it might never end.

'Come on, for fuck's sake!'

At that, Becca put her hand on the door handle again and went into the room.

'What's going on?' she asked, her voice high. Samuel was lying on the changing mat and Ryan was kneeling above him, a pile of dirty wipes beside him. He looked up.

'I was just changing him and he did an enormous shit as soon as I took the old nappy away. It's everywhere!'

I thought back to the times when this had happened to Becca, remembered her laughing and reassuring Samuel that it was all going to be okay and she would have him dry and clean in no time.

'That isn't his fault,' Becca said. 'Let me do it.'

She kneeled down, took hold of Samuel's hand. He was screaming in a way that he rarely did. It wasn't like the scream he did when he was in pain, or when he was having a tantrum. She put her other hand on his forehead and swept his hair to one side.

'It's okay, baby boy,' she said.

Slowly, gradually, Samuel calmed down. Ryan sat back on his heels.

'You do it, then,' he said, standing up and walking out of the room.

So Becca took over. Changed the nappy, found new clothes, cuddled Samuel until he was calm. 'You didn't do anything wrong,' she whispered in his ear. 'Everything is okay.'

She didn't raise it again until Samuel was having his nap after lunch.

'Why were you shouting at him when I got home?' she asked.

They were standing in the kitchen. Ryan was leaning back against the kitchen counter, waiting for the kettle to boil.

'I told you, he'd just shat everywhere! It was disgusting!'

'He's a baby, though. That's what they do.'

'He's two years old.'

Becca frowned. 'Okay, he's two. He's not potty trained, which means he doesn't have control over his bladder or bowel. It's not like he did it on purpose, to make life difficult for you…'

'You weren't here, Becca, okay? You left me looking after him so you can't come back and get all pissed off about the way I did that…'

'Er, yes, I can,' Becca said. 'I'm his mum! I'm entitled to take a bit of time for myself and also be concerned about the way he's being looked after.'

Ryan threw his hands up in exasperation. 'I know you're his mum, for fuck's sake. I'm his dad. I have a say in all this too, you know.'

I wanted her to say that he didn't, that he wouldn't, that she would leave and take Samuel and do it all her way from that moment on, and then I realised what I was wishing for and was surprised. It was the first time I'd truly wanted her to go, and to hell with the consequences for my own life. Something had switched in me. He'd gone too far. He'd frightened Samuel. He wasn't fit to be a father. Not to Samuel. Not to me.

I could see it, then, the way Lucy always had. All the

covering up I'd done for him, mentally, all the reasoning, it all fell away and I saw that he was a nasty man who didn't deserve them. Who they didn't deserve.

I looked at Lucy. She looked sad. Defeated. I wondered how to say it to her, how to tell her I'd changed my mind. But when I opened my mouth to speak, I found I couldn't do it. Not yet. Perhaps I'd have to show her, instead.

* * *

Becca swam a few more times after that, but she never left Samuel with Ryan again. Her dad stepped in, and never asked what Ryan was doing, why he couldn't be the one to take care of his son. I would have liked to watch Becca's dad and Samuel together, would have liked to see with my own eyes the things they did that Becca's dad told her about when she came back to pick him up. Train tracks, and walks to the park, even a trip to the farm. But where Becca went, I went too. So I watched her swim, saw the way her body began to change back to the one she'd had before. Her shoulders strong and muscular, her tummy tight.

When she got back to her dad's one afternoon, he asked if she had time to stay for a while and she nodded. Her hair was still wet, making a damp patch on the back of her top.

'You don't have to rush back here, you know?' her dad said, gesturing towards her long hair. 'You could dry your hair.'

'I miss him,' Becca said. 'I'm not used to being away from him.'

Her dad shrugged and handed her a mug of hot chocolate. He'd squirted cream into it, even put a few mini marshmallows on the top. He had a smaller one for Samuel. Becca grinned.

'This is a treat,' she said.

'Good. You deserve a treat.'

They went into the living room and sat down together on the sofa. Becca had put Samuel's cup on the coffee table, and he sat on a cushion on the floor, looking at a book and drinking. Becca was distracted. He couldn't be trusted yet to drink without spilling, and she was always particularly aware of this in other people's homes. She kept putting her own mug down on the floor and going over to him to help him keep his hand steady.

'Becca, sit down. He's fine. What is he going to ruin, here? You've made plenty of mess in this room, over the years. If it spills, we'll wipe it up. Have a break.'

Becca smiled. 'It's hard,' she said. 'You forget how to switch off.'

'I remember that,' her dad said, nodding. 'But it's important that you do. And here of all places, I would hope you'd feel comfortable.'

Becca sat back a little, as if to show that she was going to stay put.

'How are you?' he asked. 'I'm not trying to pry. Just wondering how things are going now, with Ryan?'

Becca usually answered these questions fast, a defensive tone in her voice. But that day she paused, looked as if she was gathering her thoughts before answering.

'I don't know, to be honest, Dad. We're supposed to be trying for another baby but I don't know whether it's the right thing. I feel like I'm doing all the hard work, with Sammy. And when he does help out, I don't necessarily agree with the way he parents him.'

Her dad was nodding.

'Was it ever like that with you and Mum?'

'Not quite like that. But we certainly had different ideas

about how to parent. I think everyone does. It's how far apart they are, and how willing you each are to compromise, that makes the difference. Your mum thought I was too soft with you, that we should discipline you more, but it just didn't make sense to me. Any time you misbehaved, I felt that you were reacting to her distance, rather than my lenience. So I just carried on doing what I was doing. Telling you I loved you. And I think it worked out fine.'

'Why was she so distant?' Becca asked.

She'd asked versions of this question before, and her dad had tried to answer, but it had never been this direct, this close to the mark. He took a sip from his mug, swallowed, fixed his eyes on hers.

'I don't know. I don't think she knows. I think if she had you now, she'd probably be diagnosed with post-natal depression. She just found it so much harder than she expected to, and we probably should have got her some help, but I didn't know how, or where to go. I let her down.'

'No,' Becca said. 'I don't think you did. You stuck around even when she wasn't the nicest person to be with. You could have left. That would have been easier.'

Her dad frowned, then. 'No, it wouldn't. Leaving her, yes, that would have made life easier. It wasn't working between us for a long time. But I couldn't leave you. That's why I stuck it out until she made the decision for both of us. You are the best part of my life, Becca. I don't regret a thing, because we had you.'

Even though I'd always known that this was how he felt, I was moved by his words. It was clear that Becca was, too. She brushed away a tear.

'Thank you,' she said. And then, after a beat of silence,

'That's how I feel about him, about Sammy. He makes it worthwhile.'

'You know you won't lose him, though, if you leave Ryan? That was my fear. Leaving and losing you. Custody was so rarely given to dads. But I don't think you'd have much of a battle on your hands with Ryan. I'm not sure he'd even fight for Sammy. I'm not trying to talk you into anything. I just want you to think about your options, because I don't think you seem very happy, and that breaks my heart.'

She wasn't happy, I thought then. She hadn't been happy for a long time. As a child, when she'd played games and made dens and watched films with her dad, then she'd been happy. Even now, she was happy with him. And Samuel made her happy, and she was with him almost all the time, so it had seemed like enough. But there were too many people in her life who weren't having that effect on her. Her mum had never been much of a mother, and Ryan wasn't much of a partner. That was all there was to it. I'd shielded myself from the truth of it for so long, but it was there, in front of me, undeniable. I felt like I'd been casting around in the fog, walking in the wrong direction, and someone had given me a torch. And I knew what I had to do.

25

JULY 2024

I didn't tell Lucy. I didn't tell anyone. Didn't dare to, in case it went wrong. The first step was to watch over Becca when she was using social media, because she and Anthony still followed each other on Instagram and I was looking for a particular post. The problem was, Becca was so busy with Samuel that she usually only gave it a quick scroll every now and again, and I knew she was missing things. I waited until she was sitting down with a cup of tea one day, Instagram open on her phone.

Look up Anthony, I thought. I was sitting right beside her. *Look up Anthony, look up Anthony, look up Anthony.*

Her finger went to the search bar, hovered there for a moment.

Look up Anthony, look up Anthony, look up Anthony.

She typed his name into the search bar, hit return. His profile loaded, and she looked at his profile photo for a moment. He was standing with a group of friends and they were throwing their mortarboards in the air. That classic, clichéd shot. He'd graduated. That was one of the things I'd wanted to know. The second was whether he was back home.

Becca scrolled down, looked at his last couple of posts. And there it was, posted three days ago. A photo of a pint, with the caption:

> Back with my parents and looking for jobs in London. Does anyone fancy a drink?

I wondered, briefly, whether he'd posted it for Becca's sake. Whether he was hoping she'd respond. She read it and then scrolled back up to the top of the screen, hit the home button. So he was back. That made what I was about to do much easier.

I wished, then, that I'd asked Samuel or Thomas or Lucy how they did it. How they slipped into the world, into another person's body. But all of them had done it, and as far as I knew there'd been no discussions about the mechanics of it with one another, so perhaps it was simple. Perhaps you just had to wish it, and it happened. I would do it the next day, I decided, or at least I would try.

That evening, Lucy was beside me. I thought about asking her, but I knew she would want to know what I'd decided to do, who I'd decided to inhabit, and I didn't want her to know. Not yet. We were mostly silent as we watched Becca make dinner and wash the dishes. When she put Samuel to bed, we sang along to 'Twinkle, Twinkle, Little Star'. It was part of their routine, and we'd both held out hope, for a long time, that it would one day be part of ours, but that hope had faded for her and it was fading for me, too. I would keep singing along with it, I thought, in case it was my only chance to duet with my mother, and help send my beloved brother off to sleep.

In the morning, I went off to a corner of the room and closed my eyes. I concentrated. I thought of Anthony, of his home on the other side of town, and I wished and waited. And then it happened. I was there, wearing his body like clothes. I put a hand up to his eyes, rubbed them, felt the drag of skin on skin. It was both exactly like I'd imagined and nothing like it. I felt a little too warm, a little tired. These were states I'd heard and wondered about so many times. What would it feel like to be cold, to be hungry, to be in pain? And I recognised them instantly, without having to be told. It was familiar, and it wasn't. It was mind-blowing. I wondered whether Lucy would have noticed that I'd gone. And then I remembered what I was there for, and that I had limited time, and I gathered myself immediately. I had to go to Becca's. I had to find her, to persuade her.

I was in Anthony's bedroom, and then I was off, down the stairs, stepping into trainers, and out of the door. It was amazing to feel the air on his skin, the warm sun on his face. I was elated, and at the same time, downcast. This was living, and it was just as wonderful as I'd always hoped it might be, perhaps more so, and this was the only chance I would get to experience it.

I walked quickly, scared that he would intervene somehow, change his mind. I didn't quite trust that I was in complete control. I was at the flat in ten minutes, banging on the door. What would I do if Ryan answered? It was unlikely, with it being a Tuesday morning. When I had left the flat, he'd gone to work, but it wasn't impossible that he might have come back for some reason. Or what if Becca's mum had called in, or more likely her dad? Again, they should have been at work, but there was an element of doubt. I heard footsteps, knew, somehow, that they were hers. And then the door was flung open and she was there in front of me, and although her face was more familiar to me than any other, it was like seeing her for the first time, this experience of looking out of another pair of eyes.

'Anthony!' she said.

It was a surprise, of course. Did she wonder about the fact that she'd searched him on Instagram the day before and now here he was, in front of her as if she'd somehow summoned him? I don't know. Samuel appeared behind her, holding onto her legs, and the impulse to reach out and touch his face was so strong that it was painful to be still.

'Can I come in?' I asked.

Unlike the last time, when she'd insisted on a trip to the park, she nodded. I was grateful to have overcome this first, tiny hurdle.

I followed her down the hallway and took in the smells of the flat I knew so well but had never truly been inside of. I marvelled over the way the laminate floor felt under my feet, the way the smell of drying washing hung in the air. I smelled something that I knew at once was coffee, and I wanted to ask her to fry some bacon or bake some bread, those smells people always talk about. I wanted to experience everything in these short hours that I had with her.

'I finished uni,' I said, then. 'Graduated. I'm back home with my parents for a while, looking for jobs.'

Becca spun around. We'd reached the living area. 'Congratulations,' she said.

There was no coldness in her tone, but there wasn't a great deal of warmth, either. I tried to focus on what she'd said to her dad, about being unsure now, in her relationship, about her doubts. *Please, Becca*, I said, internally. *Please do the right thing.*

And then I thought of Lucy, watching this happen. I looked around, wondering where she was. There, in the corner by the sofa where we sometimes stood? Or there on the floor with

Samuel? There was no way of knowing. I smiled a little to think of the way she must have reacted to this sudden appearance of her father. I wondered whether she'd noticed my absence yet, whether she'd pieced it together.

'Do you want something?' Becca asked, then.

I thought about the different ways in which I could answer. I did want something. I wanted her. I wanted her to be with him, to realise that she should have been with him all along. I wanted her to touch him and kiss him and know that he was the one for her. I wanted her to leave Ryan, and make a life with him, starting with the conception of Lucy.

'Tea, or coffee?' she asked.

'Oh,' I said. 'Coffee would be great.'

She made the drinks and I sat down on the edge of the sofa. I didn't sit down properly, because I wasn't convinced she wouldn't suddenly change, ask me to go.

'Would it be rude to ask what brings you here?' Becca asked.

'No,' I said. 'That wouldn't be rude. You've got every right to ask.'

'And?'

I tried to see it her way. She didn't know about me, or Lucy. She didn't know that the child she'd lost was called Thomas, that he was gentle and kind and would have made a wonderful brother for Samuel.

'I think about you so often,' I said. 'About that time we had, that first night and then later, those months. I've never found anything like it, before or since.'

Becca dipped her head. She was beautiful, I realised. To me, she'd always just been my mother. The most important person in the world. Her physical appearance hadn't mattered one bit. But now I could be objective, somehow, and I saw the structure of her bones beneath her skin, the length of her neck, the arrangement of her features. She was perfect.

'I'm with Ryan,' she said, but it wasn't final. It wasn't convincing.

'I don't think he treats you the way you should be treated,' I said.

I knew that there was a danger in going too fast, too strong. I made sure I didn't move closer to her. I was terrified of scaring her away.

'What do you know about my life?' she asked.

She looked at me, at him, and there were tears in her eyes. I wanted, more than anything, to reach out and wipe them away. I hadn't touched her, and I might never touch her, and I wanted her to know what she meant to me. But I stayed where I was, kept my hands on my lap. I didn't know what to say.

'I'm serious,' she said. 'You can't just appear like this because your degree is over and you're at home and you feel a bit bored. You can't just look back through your past and wonder who might still be around and willing to spend some time with you. I've been here all this time. Doing loads of washing and making endless meals for my son to throw on the floor and just being a mum, while you've been sitting in lecture theatres and getting drunk.'

She was crying properly by then.

I shifted a little nearer to her, and she didn't move away. I reached out, touched her hand. It was warm and dry, and so soft. I couldn't believe I was here with her.

'That's not what this is,' I said. 'You know I'm not like that. Come on, Becca. I've spent three years at uni and I didn't meet anyone who came close to you. I want us to give it a try, again. You, me and Samuel.'

Samuel looked over from his jigsaw puzzle at the sound of

his name. He asked for a drink, and Becca got up and went to the kitchen to get him some orange squash. I felt the lack of her hand as soon as we were no longer touching, and all I could think about was touching her again. While she was getting the drink, I slid onto the floor and helped Samuel with a piece he'd been trying to fit into the puzzle upside down. He grinned at me, and I gave him a high-five. And the touch of his skin on mine, on this skin I'd borrowed, was almost enough to make me weep. My brother. The brother I would never have.

'It's not that easy, Anthony. Ryan and I have made a life here. It's not always exciting, or exactly what I want, but I can't just keep moving Sammy from one place to another. He needs stability, and he has that here.'

'At what cost, though? Yes, stability is important, but so is happiness, and I don't believe you're happy here. I bet he isn't really, either.'

Becca handed Samuel his cup and ruffled his hair. And then she looked up, and there was venom in her eyes. 'How dare you, Anthony? I've done the best I can for him, you know? It's all I've done. I think you should leave.'

I was panicked. I was sitting on the floor with her son and she was standing in front of me, arms folded. Waiting for me to stand up and go. I had to backtrack. I'd gone too far.

'Becca, I'm sorry. I didn't mean to criticise you. You've done an amazing job with him. Just look at him. He's healthy, bright. When I said he wasn't happy, I meant with Ryan. I don't think Ryan deserves to be a dad.'

Becca's head snapped up at that. It was just what she'd been thinking lately, wasn't it? That Ryan didn't deserve the family that he had. It was what Lucy had always said, what I'd only just started to see. How had I only just started to see it? I watched Becca intently, looking for any sign of softening. I probably didn't have much time left. Why hadn't I ever asked the others how much time they'd had?

'Becca Valentine, I love you.'

It was a risk, but I had to take it. She might think it was too much, too intense, might back away from it or run away. Might push me out of the door. But I meant it. And I could feel that Anthony did too.

'You love me?' She was still crying a little, but she was smiling, too. 'Do you know that Ryan has never once said that to me?'

I was astonished. I looked back over my memories. Surely he had. What about when she'd had Samuel, or on her birthdays, or an anniversary? But she was right. I'd never heard him say those words to her.

'You deserve more,' I said. 'You deserve the whole world.'

Becca sank back onto the sofa. 'We're supposed to be trying for a baby,' she said, a little sadly.

I stood up, went back to the sofa.

'Have a baby with me instead,' I said. Then I couldn't help but burst out laughing, imagining the way Lucy would be hopping around with excitement.

'Is that a joke?' Becca asked. 'Why are you laughing?'

'Just because it's taken me so long to realise that that's what I want. It doesn't have to be now, obviously. I'm not looking to scare you. I kind of hope we might have a lifetime to think this sort of thing over.'

Becca laughed a little, too. 'I need some time,' she said.

This was tricky. I didn't want to go against what she asked for but I didn't want to waste a minute of the time I had.

'Okay,' I said. 'Whatever you need. But don't forget that I'll be waiting to hear from you.'

I leaned across the sofa towards her and gave her a gentle

kiss on the cheek. She smelled of lemons and soap, and I would have given anything to stay with her a little longer. But it was time to go. I stood up. She stood up. For a second, I thought she was going to kiss me, but then we both heard the noise at the same time, and it was unmistakeable. A key in a lock. And the only person who had a key to this flat, other than Becca, was Ryan. We both realised it at the same time and exchanged a look of panic. But it was too late to dream up an escape, to climb out of a window or hide in a wardrobe. He was already inside, his footsteps thudding down the hall.

When he opened the door to the living room, we hadn't moved a muscle. We were both standing there, inches apart, looking in his direction.

'What the fuck are you doing here?' he asked, looking straight at me.

26

JULY 2024

'Ryan,' Becca said, her voice all panic. 'It's nothing, really.'

'I'll decide if it's nothing,' Ryan said.

I stole a glance at the clock that hung on the wall opposite the sofa. I'd been here just over an hour. Plus there was the short time I'd spent at Anthony's house and walking here. But none of that meant anything because I didn't know how long you got. I could disappear at any point. But if I did, I'd leave Anthony right in the middle of this situation. I felt pretty awful about that.

I looked from one parent to the other. I wanted to tell them that I was the daughter they were never going to have. That I might look like Anthony, Becca's ex, but I wasn't, not really. I wanted to say hello, and goodbye. I wanted to tell them that it could have worked out, the three of us and Samuel, but Ryan just wasn't the right person. Just wasn't a good enough person.

'I'll tell you what it looks like, to me,' Ryan said. His voice didn't sound menacing but I knew him, knew what he was capable of. I was on my guard. 'It looks like I came home from work unexpectedly with a migraine and my girlfriend is here with her ex, looking pretty cosy. In the flat I pay for. Is that a fair summary?'

'Ryan, please—' Becca started.

I realised I hadn't said anything. 'I should go,' I said.

'I don't think so.' Ryan took a step back, so that I would have to go around him to get to the door that led out into the hallway. The only means of escape.

I began to feel uncomfortably hot. I looked at Becca, but her eyes were on him. She was pleading with him. For my sake? Or for hers? She went to pick up Samuel, who was watching what was going on, and pushed past Ryan to take him out of the room, and I was glad. When she reappeared, she had one last go at diffusing the situation.

'Ryan, nothing is going on. This is the first time I've seen Anthony in months. Please don't do anything stupid.'

'Stupid?' he asked. 'I feel like you've made me look pretty stupid, the two of you.'

It was clear that there was going to be no reasoning with him. He'd made his assumptions about what was happening, and it was too late to change his mind. I stepped towards him. What would be would be. I felt a responsibility to move things along as quickly as possible, so that it would hopefully be me, and not Anthony, who would feel the brunt of Ryan's anger.

Ryan's fist came out of nowhere and caught me on the side of the nose, and I felt a pain that was all-encompassing. So this, at long last, was the pain I'd always wondered about. It was a red-hot feeling, taking over everything else. I swallowed, tasted metal and warmth. Blood. I heard Becca scream for him to stop. And then he hit me again, and his knuckle caught my lip and I thought I might have lost a tooth, and then again, just under my ribs, and I curled in on myself before I fell. I hit the floor and saw Anthony's blood splattered there on the laminate, and all those times I'd longed to know what it was like to feel, I wanted to take them back. At that moment, being human, being alive, seemed like the worst thing in the world, and I was glad that this was going to be my only experience of it.

Ryan was kicking me then, over and over, and I wondered whether he might actually kill me. Kill Anthony. What a terrible way for this to end, if he did. I'd gone out on a limb to try to help Lucy, but getting her father killed wasn't going to do her any favours. I tried to shut it all out, the thoughts and the pain and the sound of Becca shouting his name over and over, pleading with him to stop. *Call an ambulance*, I said internally. *Call an ambulance, call an ambulance, call an ambulance.* And then I realised that I only had the ability to control her like that when I was myself, when I was in the Beforelife, and I wept. Hoped that it would be over soon, and that he wouldn't die from it.

And then I was back. No pain, no sensation at all. Lucy beside me.

'My god,' she said. 'What did you do?'

I wanted to explain, but I felt too exhausted. She didn't really think I'd tried to sabotage things, did she? Could she think that?

'Did you do that for me?' she asked.

'Yes.'

'But... why?'

'Hold on,' I said. 'I can explain it all later. Is it still going on? Is Ryan still hurting him?'

We both turned to look. It was over. Anthony was curled up on the floor, not moving, and Ryan was standing over him, breathing hard. His fists still clenched, as though he wasn't sure he'd finished. There was blood everywhere. Becca was crying, trying to pull Ryan away. And I was terrified, for a minute, that he might turn on her. That she might be next.

'Will he be okay?' I asked Lucy.

I didn't know why I thought she'd know. She gave me a blank look, said nothing.

'I'm going to call an ambulance,' Becca said, then.

'No!' Ryan spun around to face her. 'Do you know what will happen to me if you do that?'

'Look what you did to him!' Becca cried.

'Are you sleeping with him?' Ryan asked.

She shook her head, her face full of fury. 'I can't believe you...'

'Well, I can't believe you, either.' He walked out of the room, stepping over Anthony's still body, and we heard him leave the flat, slamming the door behind him.

Becca rushed to Anthony's side, kneeled down. She touched his face with such gentleness that I wished I'd been there for longer, just to feel it. Anthony opened one eye. The other one was swollen shut.

'Are you okay?' she asked through sobs.

'I thought he was going to kill me,' Anthony said. He lifted a hand to his mouth and spat some blood into it, and what looked like a tooth.

'What should I do? Should I call an ambulance?'

'Yes.'

She did, and then she called her dad at work, asked him if he could have Samuel for her. She'd never asked him before, not to leave work and help her out. He agreed without question though, must have known how much she needed him. She went to get Samuel from the bedroom, held him tight and said that she was sorry he'd seen Daddy so angry.

While they waited for her dad and the ambulance to arrive,

Becca fetched a bowl and a flannel, filled the bowl with warm water and began to wipe some of the blood from Anthony's face. He winced every time she touched him, and she kept asking if she should stop, but he gave a slight shake of his head each time and she carried on.

Her dad got there first. Becca let him in and led him into the living area. His face was a picture of shock.

'What happened here?'

He was probably imagining different scenarios. Wondering too, perhaps, whether they were having an affair.

'I'll explain it all later,' Becca said. 'I just want Samuel away from here. He shouldn't have to see any of this.'

Her dad nodded, picked up his grandson. 'Shall we go on a little adventure, my man?'

Samuel giggled as his granddad nuzzled into his neck.

'The bag with all his stuff is in the hallway, with the buggy,' Becca said.

She sounded so tired. So defeated.

'Okay,' he said. 'Call me.'

And then he was gone, and I was grateful that she had a dad like that, who stepped in when needed and didn't ask too many questions. Although the questions would all come later, I was sure of that.

Next, the ambulance arrived and the two paramedics came inside, got Anthony onto a stretcher.

'Are you coming with us?' one of them asked Becca.

She looked at Anthony, and he nodded.

'Yes,' she said. 'I'm coming.'

They walked outside, Becca pausing to lock up, and I saw her glance back at the flat and wondered whether she was saying a goodbye to it. Whatever I'd done here, I'd surely ended her relationship with Ryan. I couldn't see her going back to him now.

'So tell me,' Lucy said, once they'd loaded Anthony into the ambulance and Becca had climbed in after him and they were on their way to the hospital.

'I just... I wanted to use my Chance to help you,' I said.

I couldn't look at her, but I could feel her eyes on me. I hadn't wanted this, hadn't done it for any kind of recognition or praise. It had just felt like the obvious thing to do, once I'd realised that I couldn't push her into staying with Ryan just so I would be born.

'But what about you?' she asked.

'I just saw it, suddenly, how awful he is. I don't want to be born if it means her staying with him. It doesn't feel right.'

'I don't know what to say.'

'Well, you don't have to say anything. And I'm not sure it's helped in the end, anyway. I'm so sorry I caused that to happen to him.'

'Eliza,' Lucy said. 'You couldn't have known. What were the chances of him being ill, coming home like that? He's never home in the day. Please don't blame yourself.'

We both looked at Anthony again, then. Now that Becca had cleared his face of some of the blood, he looked a little better, or a little worse. One eye was massively swollen and his lip was cut, and he'd lost a tooth. Beyond that, we didn't know. Cracked ribs? Internal bleeding? Ryan had really gone for him, so anything was possible. The ambulance stopped, and then the back doors opened and they were lifting him out, carrying him inside. Becca followed them, and we followed her. It was just what we did.

The waiting was painful. Becca sat on an uncomfortable-looking chair in A&E for a couple of hours, while they did scans and checks and tried to determine the extent of his injuries.

'Are you his girlfriend?' one of the doctors asked at one point.

Becca looked at Anthony and I thought I saw the beginnings of a smile playing on his lips.

'Just his friend,' Becca said, and she looked so sad that I wanted to be back there, with my arms around her. I wanted to tell her that this was her chance, to be with him properly, to make it something more.

'I don't think we'll be keeping him in,' the doctor said. 'Is there someone at home who can look after him?'

'His mum,' Becca said.

And then she looked at Anthony again and it was clear that they were both thinking about how they would explain this to his parents, and to the wider world in general.

'I don't mind taking the blame,' she said, after the doctor had gone.

'What, you think I want people to believe that you did this to me?' Anthony asked.

Becca laughed a little, and then Anthony laughed, but he clutched his ribs and stopped again straight away.

'I don't mean that,' Becca said. 'I just mean... well, I don't know, really. But I feel responsible, and I'm happy to take responsibility.'

'Why?' Anthony asked, his brow furrowed.

'Because you were in my flat, and he's my boyfriend.'

We all noticed the present tense she'd used, and none of us said anything.

'Becca, what he does is not your fault. That's ridiculous.'

He sat up a little and reached to pour himself a glass of water from the jug on his tray, but every movement made him wince, so Becca took the jug from him and handed him the glass when she'd finished. He smiled at her.

'Are you going to go back to him?' Anthony asked.

I could see that it had taken a lot for him to ask it. Becca bit her lip and looked at him for a long moment.

'No, this is it. It has to be, doesn't it? I can't forgive him. Can't condone it.'

'Well, it was worth it then.'

Becca frowned. 'I'm not some sort of prize, you know?'

'I didn't mean that. Whether anything ever happens between us or not, I'm glad you won't be with him. What if he did something like this to you? Or to Sammy?'

'He wouldn't,' said Becca.

Even after today, she was quick to defend him.

'You don't know for sure. I want you both to be safe.'

Just then, a doctor appeared with a clipboard and asked if he could talk to Anthony in private, so Becca went outside, and we went with her. She walked to a vending machine and bought a flimsy plastic cup of coffee, and then burned her tongue when she tried to drink it too quickly. By the time she got back to Anthony's bedside, the doctor was gone.

'They're sending me home,' Anthony told her. 'No broken ribs. Just lots of bruising. And he asked whether I was going to press charges against the person who did it.'

'Are you?' Becca asked.

'I don't know. Whatever makes life easier for you, Becca. Do you want me to?'

She chewed on the end of a piece of hair for a moment.

'I don't care,' she said. 'I really don't care.'

27
___

JULY 2024

Becca helped Anthony to make his way outside and they got in a taxi.

'Do you want me to come in with you, when we get to your house?' Becca asked.

'No, it's fine. Becca, you're acting like you were the one who did this. Nobody is going to think it's your fault; I promise.'

She gave a quick nod and looked down. She didn't speak for the rest of the journey.

'Can you take her home now?' Anthony asked the taxi driver, handing over a twenty-pound note.

'No, no. I'll get out here,' Becca said. When he looked at her questioningly, she added, 'My dad's house is only five minutes away. Sammy's there.'

'Will you stay with him?' Anthony asked as the taxi pulled away. 'Your dad, I mean?'

'Yes. I need to go back to the flat to get our things at some point, though.'

Anthony squinted. The sun was in his eyes. I wanted Becca to put a gentle hand on his arm and turn him by ninety degrees so they could look at one another properly. But she didn't touch him, and he didn't touch her.

'Did you know that "Yesterday" has been covered more than fifteen hundred times?'

Becca looked up at him with a weak smile, one that told him she knew what he was doing, that he was trying to remind her of their early, simpler days. She didn't say anything.

'I'd better get inside,' he said.

'What will you tell your parents?'

'The truth, I guess. I'm going to press charges, Becca. I don't want to let him think he can get away with this kind of thing.'

She nodded, not happy or sad. Just resigned.

'Will you call me?' he asked. 'I don't know where you're going to be or whether you'll want to talk to me, but if you do, will you call?'

'I will.'

He leaned forward slightly and I thought he was going to kiss her on the cheek, but then he turned and went up the path to his front door.

Becca stood on the pavement as he went inside, and I wondered whether she was imagining the gasp of shock that might come from his mother when she saw the state of his face. The gasp she might make if an adult Samuel came home with one eye swollen shut and a tooth missing. Then she walked very slowly to her dad's house to pick up her little boy.

It was early evening by then, and her dad was feeding Samuel a cheese sandwich and some slices of cucumber and carrot. Samuel grinned when he saw Becca and lifted up his arms. Becca went over to the table and hugged him awkwardly, kissed the tip of his nose.

'You didn't call,' her dad said, not unkindly. 'I was wondering whether I might have him overnight.'

'Sorry,' Becca said. 'It was all just so... intense. Ambulance, hospital. They've just discharged him and I wanted to make sure he got home okay.'

'Is something going on between the two of you?' he asked. His voice was free of judgement, and I was glad.

'No,' Becca said. 'He turned up out of nowhere and said he wants to be with me. Nothing happened. But then Ryan came home and found him there, and... well, you know the rest.'

Her dad nodded. 'And where's Ryan now?'

Becca shrugged. 'No idea. At the flat, I'd guess. Anthony's going to press charges, so I imagine the police will be looking for him pretty soon.'

'And where does that leave you?'

Samuel had finished his food. Becca's dad handed him a yoghurt and a spoon, and Becca pulled out a chair and sat down next to her son.

'It's over,' she said.

Every time she said it, I dared to believe it a little bit more.

'I can't ignore something like that. Anthony thinks he could do it to me, or to Samuel. I don't think he would, but still...'

'And Anthony? How do you feel about him?'

Becca picked up a thin strip of her hair between two fingers and twisted it.

'I don't know,' she said. 'He's always been there, in the background. It's like he represents the life I could have had, if I'd chosen more wisely. But I need to put Samuel first. He needs consistency.'

Her dad nodded in agreement. He pulled out a chair and sat down, put his elbows on the table and his chin in his hands.

'Lots to think about,' he said.

'Yes.'

He leaned over and kissed the top of her head. 'Hey, I have a chocolate orange in the cupboard if you fancy helping me with it?'

Becca's face broke into a genuine smile and her dad got up to retrieve the chocolate from the cupboard. When Samuel saw it, his face was an expression of pure joy.

'Can he have a bit?' her dad asked.

Becca nodded.

They sat at the table, the three of them, saying little, eating the chocolate.

'Thanks, Dad,' Becca said.

'What for?'

'For not saying "I told you so". For not freaking out. For letting me explain it to you.'

He shrugged. 'It's what dads do, isn't it?'

And then they both looked at Samuel, and Lucy and I did, too. Not his dad.

'I'm going to go with him to the flat, pack up our things,' Becca said.

'Why don't you stay here tonight and we'll go together in the morning?'

Becca considered this.

'There are plenty of nappies and wipes in the changing bag, and he can use his change of clothes as pyjamas. And I can find you a T-shirt to sleep in.'

She nodded. 'Yes, please,' she said.

It had started to rain, and she looked out at the drops falling against the patio window, and I felt sure she was glad she didn't have to go outside again. Together, they went into the bathroom and her dad started to get Samuel undressed while Becca ran the bath and poured in the foam.

After the bath, he told her to relax in the living room while he read Samuel a story. She kissed Samuel, and he wrapped his legs around her and gave her a long cuddle.

'Where Daddy?' he asked.

Becca and her dad exchanged a look.

'I'm not sure, baby. He did something wrong today and we might not be able to see him for a little while.'

'I see you?' he asked, frowning.

'You will always see me,' she said, pulling him a tiny bit tighter and letting him nestle into her shoulder. 'Always. Now, Granddad's going to read you a story and put you to bed, and I'll be in a bit later, okay?'

'For cuddles.'

'Yes, please.'

She retreated into the living room and sat down on the sofa, brushing away tears. She sent a couple of messages. One to Ryan:

> Sammy and I are staying at Dad's tonight, and then I'll come and pick up some stuff tomorrow.

She stared at her screen for a few minutes, but no reply came. Then she sent one to Anthony:

> Are you okay? I keep thinking about your face, about the pain you were in. I never want to see anything like that again.

And almost straight away, he responded.

> I'm okay. Mum went nuts. We talked to the police. They haven't been able to find Ryan yet, so I'm guessing he's not at the flat. It's nice to hear from you, Becca Valentine. And don't forget the things I said.

Not at the flat? That was odd. I wondered where else he might go. To his parents? They weren't especially close. Perhaps he was running away from the responsibility of it. After all, when he'd left it hadn't been clear how serious Anthony's injuries were.

Her dad came back into the room, then. 'He's all snuggled up. I said one of us would check on him in five minutes but I'll be surprised if he's not asleep by then. We went to the park this afternoon and he ran around for ages. He's shattered.'

'Thanks, Dad,' Becca said. 'Listen. I just heard from Anthony. He said the police couldn't find Ryan, so it sounds like he's not at the flat. I might just go there now and grab some stuff, to save me running into him tomorrow. Do you mind staying here with Sammy? I'll wait until he's asleep.'

'I don't mind at all,' her dad said. 'But are you sure you want to go alone?'

'Yes, it's fine. If he's there, I'll just leave.'

Her dad kept his eyes on her. He was trying to decide what he should and shouldn't allow, I thought. But his daughter had been living with this man for a long time, had a child with him. It was a little too late to insist on her not seeing him.

'Okay.'

* * *

On the short walk to the flat, Lucy spoke up. 'I don't like this,' she said.

I didn't either, but I didn't know whether echoing her worries would be helpful.

'Do you think he'll be there?' I asked.

'I hope not.'

Things felt altered between us. It felt like we'd been

opposed for a long time, wanting different things, and now, we were aligned. I felt sure that had to mean something. That together, we stood more hope of achieving it.

When she got to the flat, Becca let herself in and pushed the door open. And I was sure, as soon as she did, that he was there. Even before he came out into the hallway, his face grim. Even before he called out, 'Becca, is that you? I've been waiting for you.'

28

JULY 2024

Becca froze in the doorway, and I hoped she might turn and go straight back out again, but then he was there, coming towards her.

'I thought you weren't here,' she said quietly.

'Who told you that? Your lover?'

He said the word with a sneer. It was hard to tell, from his expression, whether he was scared or angry or a combination of the two.

'The police are looking for you,' she said.

His face fell. Perhaps he'd counted on Becca talking Anthony out of that. I was glad she hadn't, but I was scared, too. I hoped she wouldn't end up being punished somehow.

'Anyway, I'm just here to pick up some things for me and Sammy. I don't want to have an argument.'

Ryan followed her into the bedroom, watched her as she pulled a rucksack from the wardrobe and began to fill it with clothes and toiletries.

'You're leaving me over this?' Ryan asked. 'What about the baby?'

Becca spun around. 'What baby?'

'The baby we were planning. You could be pregnant right now; we don't know.'

A look of horror crossed Becca's face as she realised it could be true. I knew it wasn't, and I wished I could tell her.

'I'm not pregnant, and I'm not going to be. I don't want to do this, with you.'

I already knew, of course, that my chance was gone, but this was the first time I'd heard her say it, and it stung. Lucy looked across at me with sympathy in her eyes, and I knew that if we had bodies, if we had hands, we would have held them.

'Becca, you can't just throw it all away because—'

'Because you assaulted someone? Because you were prepared to let our son see you punch and kick someone until he needed an ambulance? I think I can, thanks.'

She'd finished packing, the rucksack full of hastily chosen items, but full, nonetheless. She went to the door. Ryan put his arms across the doorframe, blocked her way.

I looked at Becca, tried to assess whether she was scared. How scared she was. She was breathing heavily, but she looked more angry than anything else. Perhaps seeing him at his worst, seeing the violence unleashed, had snapped something in her. Perhaps she knew he wouldn't go for her the way he went for Anthony. But when she pushed past him for the second time that day, I thought, for a second, that he might. He balled his hands into fists, shouted her name.

'Becca, don't go!'

'It's too late for that,' she said over her shoulder. 'Did you really think I'd stay with you after what you did? Do you know me at all?'

I thought about that. Catalogued the wrongs he'd done, the ones she'd stayed with him through. She'd stayed when he'd pushed her and she'd lost Thomas. She'd stayed when she'd caught him shouting unnecessarily at their son. But she wouldn't stay with him now that he had assaulted her friend, her ex. Did that mean something? Perhaps she was in love with Anthony, after all. Or perhaps it was just the last straw. Maybe all those things had built and built and now there was a wall between them that was too high to see over, or to knock down.

When she pulled the door behind her, I was flooded with relief. But a moment later, he opened the door and came out into the night, calling her name.

'Don't you get it?' she asked, turning. There were tears in her eyes. 'It's over. I don't love you, Ryan. I can't. Not after seeing you do something like that.'

'Is it because of him?' Ryan asked, most of the aggression gone from his voice, replaced with sadness.

'No, not really. I mean, I don't know. Maybe. But I couldn't have stayed with you no matter who you did that to. I can't bring Sammy up in a home where that kind of thing can happen.'

Ryan looked down at his socked feet. 'You and Sammy can stay here, for now.'

Becca started to shake her head, to tell him he didn't understand.

'No,' he insisted. 'I'll go. I'll pack some things and disappear tonight. You said the police are looking for me. I don't fancy my chances. Will you do one thing for me? Will you say you haven't seen me, that you don't know where I am?'

Becca looked up at him, wide-eyed. 'You're asking me to lie to the police?'

'It's only a small thing. Just give me a head start. Say you never saw me after I left you and Anthony here.'

Say no, I thought. *Say no, say no.* I repeated it, over and over.

'Okay,' she said. 'But if you're here in the morning when Sammy and I come back...'

'I won't be. Thank you, Becca.'

He reached out to take hold of her hand, and I'll never know whether he was going to try to pull her to him or just touch her for the last time, because she pulled away and turned to leave. And that time, she didn't look back.

* * *

Life went on much as before. It wasn't unusual for Becca to do all the childcare, all the relentless cleaning and making of meals. The only difference was that, in the evening, Ryan didn't come home. Sometimes her dad came over and made dinner, to give her a break and some company. Anthony stayed away, for a while. He sent a lot of messages, and Becca sent a lot back, but he didn't come over. He said he was trying to give her some space, and I think she appreciated that, although I also knew that if he'd turned up on the doorstep, she would have been happy to see him.

He'd asked, early on, about Ryan disappearing. He'd asked her straight out whether she'd seen him when she went to the flat. And Becca had looked at his message for a long time before replying. And when she did, it said:

No, he was gone.

I don't know whether Becca kept expecting to hear a key in the lock, to hear Ryan letting himself in, but I did. And I suspected she did, too, because she never seemed able to fully relax. Her dad commented on it more than once. Asked if they'd be happier staying at his.

'I love it at yours,' Becca said. 'Samuel does too. But it's kind of sad for me there, too. So many memories from my childhood, stuff with Mum...'

'Have you seen much of her?' her dad asked, leaning forward.

Becca shook her head. 'We don't really work, Mum and me. We never have. It was okay when it was the three of us. I could pretend that things were fine. But when it's just me and her, it's so obvious that there isn't much between us. And I can't just go on like I always have, hoping it will change. It's too painful. I think it's time to accept that this is how things are.'

They were sitting at the table, having just eaten beans on toast. Her dad pulled his chair a little closer to Becca's and put an arm around her shoulder. 'I know,' he said. 'I understand.'

After a pause, he spoke again. 'Things were so different, back then. People didn't talk the way they do now. If you couldn't connect or bond with your baby, you just kept it a secret. She never really told me how she felt. But I could see, as you were growing up; there was just something missing. I'm sorry it was like that for you.'

Becca had tears in her eyes. I thought about the way she showed Samuel every day that she loved him, how she picked him up and kissed him when he fell, how she got up in the night when he called her, no matter how tired she was. Ryan didn't do any of those things, just like her own mum hadn't. Her dad had done all of that, for Becca. Perhaps having one devoted parent was enough.

'Thank you,' she said. 'I feel like now I'm a mum myself, I sort of understand it a bit better. She just didn't take to it. It's hard, isn't it? And it wasn't right for her. It's sad but there's nothing any of us can do about it now.'

It was one thing understanding it, in a theoretical way, but quite another to live it. And Becca's tears told a story of their own.

'I had you,' she said, then. 'I'm so glad I had you. Thank you for everything.'

Her dad brushed away tears. 'Thank you,' he said. 'Raising you was the greatest pleasure of my life. And now we have Sammy, and being able to be involved is like being given a second chance.'

'I'd like to have another one,' Becca said. 'It was lonely, being an only one. I'd like to give him a companion.'

Her dad nodded. 'Well, here's hoping for that.'

Lucy and I shared a look. Becca had two more chances to become a mother. Just two. There was no waiting for a few years and seeing what happened with her life and her relationships. She could conceive me in a few weeks' time, with Ryan, who she didn't love. Who had left and could be anywhere. Or she could conceive Lucy, in a few months, with Anthony. Anthony, who I suspected she did love; who I was pretty sure loved her. Who was living a few minutes away, and who was at the end of a phone line, and who was all the things Ryan was not. Reliable, caring, kind. And Lucy and I had done all we could, or thought we had, and now all that was left was to wait.

29

SEPTEMBER 2024

As my days ran down, the sand in the timer all but gone, everything felt so precious. All those years I'd had, first the four of us, then me, Lucy and Thomas waiting for Samuel to be born and then delighting in watching him grow, and then more recently, just Lucy and me. We'd both wasted time trying to push our own agendas, her ranting over what a terrible person Ryan was and me desperately hoping Becca and Ryan would stay together long enough for me to be conceived. It felt like all of those years were compressed into a few minutes, and I had seconds left.

I felt panicky, the way I imagine you'd feel if you were diagnosed with something terminal and you only had a matter of weeks or months to tell all the people in your life what they had meant to you. But at least in that scenario, you would have lived. And you would have access to those people. The only person I could speak to was Lucy. I couldn't reach Becca, who I'd hoped for all those years would become my mother. I couldn't reach Samuel. Or I could, but not in any meaningful way. I struggled with that. I'd broken that membrane between worlds, but for what? What did it matter, if I couldn't make anything significant happen?

I started to follow Becca everywhere. I'd always been with her a lot, but I'd take breaks when she was sleeping or doing something I wasn't interested in watching. But in those final days, I watched her every second. I sat with her while she watched television, while she ate breakfast, while she showered. And any time she wasn't with Samuel, I felt a wrench and willed her to go back to him. I tried to drink them both in. Tried to do the impossible, to stretch time. And even as I tried, time contracted, squashed in and folded over. A day of Becca playing with Samuel, taking him to playgroup and then to the library, seemed like a mere hour. I despaired, watched the clock more than I should have done. I prayed. For time. For something to change.

On my last Tuesday, I sat beside Samuel as he raced cars up and down the living room, chased after them with him. Imagined we were truly side by side. Brother and sister. The way it might have been.

'I'm Eliza,' I said, over and over. 'Do you remember, Samuel? From the Beforelife? I love you, and I'm sorry I can't come to join you. I wish I could stay here forever, watching you grow up, but my time is running out. On Saturday, I'll disappear. It wasn't meant to be, you and me being together in the world. Tasting the same foods, sitting side by side on our first rollercoaster, shrieking with laughter as we played together. It wasn't meant to be. You'll have Lucy for all that, I hope, and she loves you too. Just, not quite like this. Not quite like me. Eliza.'

'Za,' Samuel said. And then he stood up. 'Li-za.'

Becca was making a cup of tea. 'What are you saying, Sammy? What is it?'

'Li-za.'

I should have been elated, but what was the good of getting through to him now, with mere days to go? I should have worked harder on it, when I had longer. Perhaps I could have worked out a way to use it for good, this ability I'd honed. But it was too late. It was all too late. I could feel time closing in on me, everything closing down.

'Liza?' Becca said, frowning. 'We don't know any Lizas, Sammy.'

They didn't, and they never would.

* * *

On Wednesday, Becca and Samuel baked fairy cakes together and ate them after his nap, and Becca's dad came round for tea and put Samuel to bed so Becca could have a bit of a break. I spent this break with her, beside her on the sofa, wishing I could smell the crook of her neck the way I did when I was there beside her. Remembering her scent, of lemon and soap. She was reading a book, and I looked at the words on the page, trying to experience them the way she was. And then her phone buzzed, and she pulled it out of the pocket of her jeans and saw that it was a message from Anthony. She smiled. She always smiled when she heard from him.

> Hey, Becca Valentine, how are you and Sammy doing? I miss you. Can we go on a date, please? I'd love to take you out for dinner on Sunday, if you can get a babysitter.

She didn't reply straight away. I thought she was probably waiting for her dad to emerge from the bedroom so she could ask if he was free to have Samuel for a sleepover on Sunday. She kept looking at the message, reading it over and over. She left her book face-down on the sofa, forgotten. When her phone buzzed again, she looked surprised. Did she think he might have had a change of heart, or that he wanted to ask her something else? She picked it up, furrowed her brow. But it wasn't another message from Anthony. It was a message from Ryan. The first time she'd heard from him since they'd said goodbye on the street outside this flat two months before, her promising not to tell the police that she'd seen him.

> Becca, can I see you? Can I come over on Saturday? Please say yes. I know what I've done and I'm not going to try to persuade you to take me back. I just need to talk to you about things. And I want to see Sammy.

Again, she put her phone down. It was as though she thought the messages would go away if she didn't look at them. It wasn't her usual way, avoidance. But perhaps she genuinely didn't know what to do. These two men, both pulling her in opposite directions. Anthony wanting to start something with her, and Ryan possibly wanting to pick things back up again, despite what he'd said about that not being the case. I knew him well enough by now to know that his message could well be full of lies. That he wasn't beyond trying to trick her into getting back together with him.

'Saturday,' Lucy said, urgently. 'He wants to come over on Saturday.'

I looked at her, confused. Unsure what her point was.

'That's your day, Eliza!' she said.

She was right. I'd put it behind me so completely, the chance of being conceived, that I'd just started seeing Saturday as my last day, nothing more.

'She wouldn't...' I said.

Lucy didn't look convinced. 'What if she does?'

I didn't answer. We both knew the answer without me saying it. If she let him in, if they, by some miracle, slept together, then there was a chance I would be conceived. And if I was, it wasn't my countdown we were living through, but Lucy's.

Neither of us said much while Becca sat through dinner with her dad. She didn't so much as glance at the phone, and it didn't buzz again, and it seemed like she'd forgotten about those messages, though we knew she couldn't have done.

Only later, when her dad had kissed her on the top of the head and gone home, did she pick her phone up again. She flicked between the messages, looking at both of them for a long time. And then she replied. First, to Anthony.

> Hi, I'm sorry but I still need some more time. I promise to message you when I'm ready.

Lucy's face twisted as the words formed on the screen.

'She's changing her mind,' she said. 'She's going to go back to Ryan again.'

'I don't think so,' I said. 'Try not to worry.'

Try not to worry was the most pointless of things to say. We'd heard it said so many times, when people were ill, when children were missing, when jobs were at risk. It was always said in situations where people couldn't help but worry, and this was no exception. How could Lucy ignore all of this? She had nothing to do but watch it play out, and despite all the evidence that Anthony was the man for Becca and Ryan was not, she did seem to be acting strangely. As if she wasn't quite sure. As if she wanted to give things with Ryan one final chance.

We watched, rapt, as she sent a reply to Ryan.

Okay, Saturday.

No kisses, no niceties, no indication of her feelings. I looked at the clock, watched a full minute tick by. Each one, each minute, was a reminder that I was on limited time, that it was all slipping away faster than I could grab it. I turned to Lucy and tried to convey what I felt, all of it. All the fear, the love, the hope, the worry. And I saw all of those things reflected back at me. And I wished, harder than I'd ever wished for anything, that we could both get a chance. That we could be sisters.

30

SEPTEMBER 2024

The days sped by. I tried to cling to them, but time slips away, no matter how much you want it to stop. It was Saturday. There had been a few more messages between Ryan and Becca, but she had never ventured into being chatty. Never asked him where he'd been, or whether he was still running from the police. There was no way of knowing how things were going to go down when she saw him, but there was no indication that she'd forgiven him either. That she was willing to give things another go. I was clinging onto that, and so was Lucy.

That morning, Becca cleaned the flat. Samuel had a toy Hoover and he followed her around the place, telling her he was getting all the bits she'd missed. She laughed and lifted the Hoover's nozzle, pretended she was going to suck him up with it. Samuel shrieked and ran away, and she chased after him and picked him up and spun him around, and for a minute, the cleaning was forgotten. By lunchtime, though, she'd managed to clean the kitchen and the bathroom and she'd Hoovered and dusted throughout, despite Samuel's near-constant distractions.

This was what she did. What single mothers do. She took care of her child and she took care of the place where they lived. It was relentless work, I'd realised. She rarely sat down. She spent all day playing and tidying and cooking, and it didn't stop when she put him down at night. Once he was asleep, she often started again, doing the things she hadn't got around to doing during the day. She was a hero. The hardest-working person I knew. And the work was thankless, and it didn't pay.

It wasn't sustainable long-term, this living arrangement. Lucy had said that, and I'd realised she was right. Becca didn't earn any money, and who knew how long Ryan would pay the rent, especially if he was absent from work, trying to evade the police. I wondered how much that played on Becca's mind. Whether that was what she was going over on the nights she lay awake, staring at the ceiling. Perhaps that's why she'd agreed to Ryan coming over that day. Perhaps she just needed to know where she stood, and what was going to happen. She'd called her dad the week before, checked that it was okay for her and Samuel to move in if they needed to. Knowing it was. She had a back-up plan.

Becca and Samuel ate tuna sandwiches and carrot sticks and crisps for lunch. I tried to notice every single thing she did for him, every touch of his hair, every quick, impromptu hug. And all the things he did to make her laugh. The faces he pulled and the way he misunderstood things, like when he asked if his friend Matty from playgroup could be their pet. There was so much love between them. It was going to make up for everything he was missing out on in a father. Even if Becca remained single for the rest of Samuel's childhood, and he only ever knew one parent, she was going to be enough. And if she got back together with his father, with Ryan... Well, it was impossible to say what would happen then, but still, this solid foundation of love was all I could hope for, for him.

Ryan was due to arrive at one o'clock. At ten to, there was a knock on the door. It wasn't his usual hammering. It was tentative. I thought perhaps it was the postman. But when Becca pulled the door open, there he was. He'd smartened up a little. Had a haircut and a shave. He was wearing his best jeans and a shirt Becca had given him for Christmas. And on his face, a look of repentance. And I knew, then, what this was. It was a seduction, an apology, an attempt to charm her. It was just what Lucy and I had feared.

'Come in,' Becca said, standing back.

'Thank you.'

He stepped inside and their bodies were close in the narrow hallway. They both looked uncomfortable, and Becca stepped away, turned and led the way to the kitchen and living room. It was so strange to think that they had been partners, lovers, until so recently. That they were co-parents. That they had talked about having another child. Having me. When Ryan saw Samuel, he reached out his arms but Samuel didn't run into them.

'Sammy, come on,' he said. 'It's Daddy.'

Samuel frowned and I felt a flutter of excitement. Perhaps he would be the one to stop it all. Slowly, he walked over and accepted Ryan's hug, but he didn't hug back, didn't nuzzle his face into the crook of Ryan's neck, the way he always did with Becca.

'I've brought you something,' Ryan said, then.

He was carrying a plastic bag, and he took a toy digger out of it, and Samuel's face lit up. It was like a toy he played with endlessly, but much bigger. I could already imagine him putting his small treasures, paperclips and buttons and marbles, in the scoop. While Samuel was distracted by this offering, Becca put the kettle on, and Ryan asked for a coffee. Everything felt a little awkward, a little stilted, as though they were strangers.

'Did the police find you?' Becca asked.

Ryan looked up and inhaled sharply. He obviously hadn't expected her to ask that, and neither had I. Perhaps she was stronger than we all gave her credit for.

'No,' he said. 'I mean, he's okay, right? I don't suppose they wasted too much time looking for me.'

'It depends on what you mean by okay,' Becca said, looking directly at him over the kitchen counter. 'You didn't break any ribs but he was badly bruised, he lost a tooth and his eye was swollen shut for over a week.'

Ryan's expression shifted a little at those last few words. 'You're in touch with him, then?'

'Yes.'

'Are the two of you together?'

Becca didn't answer straight away. She let him wait. 'Why should I tell you that? You'll probably make your own mind up anyway. That day you hurt him, I told you nothing was going on and you didn't believe me.'

'I know,' Ryan said, standing up from where he'd sat on the edge of the sofa like a guest who wasn't sure whether he was welcome. 'I was completely out of order. But look at it my way. I came home unexpectedly and found him here with you...'

'That's not the point. None of that matters. I told you it was nothing and you didn't believe me. And then you behaved like an animal, in front of your son. I had to take him out of the room so he didn't see what Daddy was doing to Mummy's friend. It was totally out of order.'

Ryan nodded and said nothing. There was no defence. I was

glad to see he didn't try to come up with one. Instead, he got
down on the floor next to Samuel and began to play with him.
Samuel had the new digger, was pulling it back and forwards
across the floor, and Ryan picked up a tractor and tried to drive
it alongside Samuel's vehicle. But Samuel kept pushing the
tractor away, and eventually Ryan gave up and just sat and
watched him. When Becca brought his coffee over, he took it
from her and said thank you, and when she sat down on the
sofa, he got up and joined her.

'I miss him,' he said simply.

'Of course,' Becca said. 'I mean, you can see him...'

'He's changed, you know, since I last saw him. His face is
getting slimmer and he's looking less like a baby.'

Becca looked at her son, tilted her head. I thought it was
probably true, what people said, about you not noticing
changes in people you saw regularly. Becca was with Samuel
every day, and the changes in him were slow and slight. She
didn't see them. We didn't either. But now Ryan had said it, I
tried to look at him objectively and I saw that he was a little boy
now, that his chubby baby cheeks were gone and his legs were
getting longer. I didn't know how Ryan could be in the same
room with him and not reach out to hold him. If only I had one
more chance, one more opportunity.

Quite unexpectedly, Ryan leaned forward and put his hand
on the back of Becca's head and kissed her. It took Becca a
second or two to react, but when she did, she pulled away.

'No!' she said, more firmly than I'd expected. 'You can't do
that, Ryan. You said you wanted to talk and see him. You can't
just kiss me.'

Ryan sat back. He looked deflated. He was used to getting
what he wanted, I thought. Especially with her. Perhaps that's
why he'd gone for someone so young. So that he could manip-

ulate her, control her to an extent. She'd said no to him before, but not so often. Not as often as an older partner might have done.

'I thought, if we talked, you might change your mind,' he said.

It was a voice I'd heard him use many times before. I'd always thought it was quite sweet. That day, it sounded pathetic, wheedling.

'No,' she said again. 'That's not going to happen.'

I looked across at Lucy and the relief was clear in her eyes, but she flashed an apologetic look at me. It wasn't necessary. I'd accepted this. I wanted this. I was on her side now.

'Are you with him?' Ryan asked. 'Are you going to be?'

Becca flushed slightly. 'I don't know yet,' she said.

Ryan nodded, reached for his mug of coffee.

'It's not just him I miss,' he said.

Please, Becca, I thought. *Stay strong. Don't be charmed. Don't waver.*

'We need to talk about stuff,' Becca said, ignoring his comment. 'We need to decide what's going to happen with the flat. Where have you been living?'

Ryan shrugged, as if he didn't know and had no interest. 'Just staying with friends.'

'I can't afford to pay the rent on this place, and I don't know what your plans are...'

Ryan stood up. 'Come on, Becca. We don't need to get into all that right now. Relax a bit. Let's have a drink.'

He went to the fridge and came back with two bottles of beer that had been in there since he'd left. He handed one to Becca. She looked unsure, but she took it.

* * *

An hour later, they were both on the floor, rolling a ball to Samuel and watching him catch it between his legs. He was giggling, overjoyed. Becca was smiling, more relaxed. I was tense as hell.

'I can't believe I'm spending my last day feeling like this,' I said to Lucy.

'I know,' she said. 'It's not fair. You know, there are things I want to say...'

I'd wondered whether she would do this. Whatever happened now, this day was goodbye for us. Either one of us would be conceived, or neither of us, and perhaps there was another world that you went to if you didn't make it, and perhaps we'd meet Thomas there, but it was a long shot and we had to assume this was the end.

'I wish things were different,' she said.

I nodded. I believed her. Why couldn't we all have had Anthony as our father, all had conception dates a couple of years apart, when Becca was in her twenties or thirties? We could have had brilliant lives, and so could she. None of the heartache and confusion. None of the pain. It was a fairytale, of course. We'd seen enough of life in our years of watching to know that no one escaped without any pain. But it could have been better. I really believed that.

'I hope it works out for you,' I said. 'I hope Becca and Anthony get it together in time.'

Lucy smiled, but it didn't reach her eyes. 'It could still work out for you instead, just about.'

We looked over at the family scene in front of us. Ryan had a hand on Becca's arm, showing her how to throw the ball towards a little toy basketball hoop he'd set up in the corner, and she was smiling. It was three in the afternoon. There was a tiny flicker of hope within me, but I extinguished it, reminded myself that this scene wasn't the way things would be. That this reunion wasn't in Becca's best interests, or Samuel's, or Lucy's. Only Ryan's. And mine, of course.

'I love you, Eliza. I don't think I've ever said that. I've loved these years with you. I'm sorry things haven't always been easy between us.'

Something inside me started to ache. I loved her too. Why had we never told each other?

'Thank you,' I said. 'I love you, too. And I love her. If you remember any of this... I mean, I know you won't, but if by any chance you do, please give her all of the love that I can't. And Samuel, too.'

We looked at Samuel. At his happy, perfect face. He ran to Becca and pushed his head into her tummy and she wrapped her arms tight around him and I imagined I could feel it. Her warmth, her love. I imagined it was me she was holding.

31

SEPTEMBER 2024

Ryan offered to put Samuel to bed and I tried to remember whether he'd ever done that before. He was trying to show her that he could be different, that he could change. But I didn't believe he could, not really. The odd bedtime, the odd afternoon playing as a family, it wasn't real. It wasn't enough. It wasn't anything near to what Anthony was offering her. I hoped she was smart enough to remember that.

When he came back into the room, he handed Becca another beer.

'Is he asleep already?' she asked.

'Yes, he was shattered. He fell asleep in the middle of me reading a story.'

Becca smiled, had a drink. 'This has been nice,' she said.

'What has?'

'This afternoon, the three of us being together.'

Ryan smiled. 'It has, hasn't it?'

If I'd had breath, I would have held it.

He slid along the sofa towards her, and she didn't do anything to stop him. He put his hand on her hair, put his beer down on the floor and took hers from her, put that down too. And while I waited for him to kiss her, waited to see what she would do, or say, I thought about the first time he'd kissed her, three years ago at a party. So much had happened since then, and so much of it was bad. I couldn't look at Lucy, couldn't see the pain and disappointment that would surely be plain to see in her eyes. I couldn't look away, either. Ryan edged closer, and Becca's face took on an expression I couldn't quite make out. And then he kissed her, and she didn't lean into it, but she didn't push him away either. He put his hands on her, one on her back and the other on the back of her head, and it felt territorial. It felt wrong.

They broke apart and Becca put her hands on his shoulders. 'No,' she said quietly.

'Come on.' Ryan kissed her again, and there was nothing gentle or romantic about it. It was like an exchange. Like something being taken.

Again, Becca pulled away. 'Ryan, stop,' she said.

But he lunged for her again, pulled her towards him with both hands, and suddenly I knew that he wasn't going to stop, that he had no intention of stopping, that he was here to take what he wanted and he didn't care how she felt about that.

I moved to the doorway. It was as far as I could go from her. I stood there and I shouted as loud as I could.

'SAMUEL! WAKE UP, SAMUEL! SAMUEL!'

'What are you doing?' Lucy asked, her voice all fear.

I didn't answer, couldn't. Wasn't it obvious? I was trying to stop it.

'SAMUEL! SAMUEL! SAMUEL!'

I heard him, then. Heard his feet thud to the floor and his footsteps patter to the doorway of the bedroom. I glanced across at the scene on the sofa. Ryan was trying to pull off

Becca's top and she'd gone quiet and still. She was playing dead, I realised, the way Samuel did sometimes. She'd probably left her body, in her mind. She was waiting for it to be over, no fight left.

And then Samuel was in the room, his hair in disarray and his fists curled, rubbing at his bloodshot eyes.

'Mummy?' he called.

It all stopped in an instant. Ryan took his hands and his mouth away from Becca, and she stood up hastily.

'What is it, Sammy?'

He shrugged.

'Can't sleep?'

He shook his head. Becca picked him up and carried him back to the bedroom, casting a look over her shoulder on her way out of the room.

'Go, or I'll call the police,' she said quietly.

Lucy and I went with her to the bedroom. It was dark in there, the only light coming from Samuel's duck-shaped nightlight. I couldn't see whether she was crying. Her clothes were rumpled. She sat down on the edge of the bed. Samuel wrapped his arms tight around her.

'I love you, baby,' she said, kissing the top of his head.

'Love you, Mama.'

She rocked back and forth with him until he was almost asleep, and then she stood and laid him down in his little bed. She sat back down, held his hand for a minute or two. And then we all heard it. Ryan's footsteps, coming out of the living room. He was either leaving or he was coming into the bedroom. Becca froze. She dropped Samuel's hand and I waited for him to cry in indignation, but he was already asleep again and he just shuffled a bit and rolled over. The footsteps got louder, stopped for a moment. He was standing on the other side of the door. Becca didn't move, didn't speak. And then they started up again, and he was moving down the hall and away. We heard the door open and then slam shut. He was gone.

I felt a rush of emotions like a wave. It was over, done. Becca's ordeal, but also my last sliver of hope. As much as I'd tried to rid myself of it, to plough everything I had into wishing for things to go Lucy's way, a sliver had remained. I couldn't help it. It was like Samuel had said, once. It was built into us, the drive to exist. It was just part of nature. I felt Lucy shuffle closer, knew that she was offering her condolences.

'It's for the best,' I said.

'I know. It doesn't make it hurt any less, though.'

There was a lifetime of kindness in Lucy's eyes.

'Look after Samuel,' I said.

She laughed. 'If I make it, I'll be his little sister. He'll be looking after me.'

'You'll make it,' I said. 'And I hope you'll look after each other.'

'Thank you.' Her voice had changed, turned serious and choked. 'Thank you for what you did just now, for stopping it. I never thought, all those hours you spent trying to communicate with them, that it would change everything like that.'

'It was the right thing to do, that's all.'

'But that doesn't mean that everyone would have done it.'

It didn't; she was right. But I'd learned something, in all those years of watching and waiting. I'd learned that doing the right thing, the kind thing, is more important than anything else. Even if it means shooting yourself in the foot. Even if it means you will never get to live at all.

I thought back to those hours I'd spent in this flat, in Anthony's body. I closed my eyes and tried to remember the way it had smelled, the everyday sounds of the toilet flushing and

Samuel's toys squeaking. Most of all, I tried to remember the way Becca's skin had felt, when I'd touched her. And the way she'd looked up at me, when she'd thought I was Anthony. The love there. All the love.

Becca was taking her clothes off, pulling on her pyjamas. She brushed her teeth, had a wee. She looked defeated, worn out. I wished we had some way of telling her that it was going to be okay, that Ryan was out of her life now. I hoped that was true. It was strange watching her get ready for bed like that, knowing it was the last time. I stared at her in the mirror above the sink, tried to make her see me, knowing she couldn't. How do you say goodbye to someone who's been your whole world when they don't know you? When you realise for sure that they never will? You don't. You can't. You just soak up the last little bit of time you have with them, watch them sleep. Curl up beside them. And wait.

EPILOGUE
DECEMBER 2024

Becca walked slowly through town in the rain, an umbrella held above her head. Samuel was in the buggy, rain cover fixed in place. He was poking and prodding at it, ready to be free. He was getting too big for it, really, but he still wasn't keen on walking far or on holding hands. It was the Saturday before Christmas and the pavements were crowded with last-minute shoppers. Samuel pointed at lights and decorations, the magic of Christmas just starting to mean something to him.

When they reached the café, Becca pushed the door open with the buggy and stepped inside.

Anthony was waiting for her at a table. When he saw her, he jumped up and took her umbrella, helped to take the rain cover off and release the straps that held Samuel in place.

'Hey, little guy,' he said, and Samuel broke into a grin, then stood up and dashed off to the counter to choose the cake Becca had promised him.

'Thanks for meeting me,' Anthony said, looking at Becca.

His eye was healed, his nose slightly wonky, but not too

much. If you hadn't known about the fight, you wouldn't guess. He looked like his old self.

Becca smiled, wide and genuine. 'I'm sorry I made you wait so long. I just had to be sure.'

'And are you?'

But before she could answer, Samuel shouted, 'Mama! Time for cake.'

Becca laughed, and Anthony laughed, and they went over to him and looked at the biscuits in the shape of hearts and cupcakes with gummy sweets sitting on top of the icing. Samuel pointed to the cupcakes, said he wanted the one with the teddy on it. The woman behind the counter pulled it out with a pair of tongs and put it on a plate.

'Anything else?' she asked.

They ordered drinks, and Becca chose a heart-shaped shortbread biscuit and told Anthony she would share it with him. When Anthony took the plates over to the table, the woman behind the counter winked at Becca.

'What a great dad,' she said.

They both looked over. Anthony was lifting Samuel onto a chair, pushing him in close to the table. Samuel put his hand up and Anthony gave him a high-five.

'Oh, he's not...' Becca started. And then she shook her head. 'Thanks.'

* * *

When they were all sat down, Anthony cleared his throat.

'I have news,' he said. 'While I've been waiting for you to make up your mind, I've been keeping myself busy. I've got a new job in London; I started last week. I'm on a graduate scheme at an IT consultancy.'

Becca smiled. 'That's amazing,' she said. 'Well done.'

'I haven't finished yet. I've also had enough of living with my parents, so I used the money I've saved since finishing uni to put a deposit down on a flat.'

'Near here, or...?' Becca asked. Her face had fallen.

'It's here. Just around the corner. The train into London only takes half an hour, and the office is only a couple of stops on the Tube from Waterloo. It's nice, Becca. Small, but almost new. I'm just trying to get myself sorted out. To make sure I'm the kind of person you might want to be with.'

Samuel had finished his cake and had icing all around his mouth, so Becca rooted around in the changing bag for a wipe. 'You're already the kind of person I want to be with,' she said. 'With Ryan, it was nothing to do with him being more stable, having a place to live...'

'I know. It was about him being Sammy's dad.'

'And now he's lost that right,' Becca said, her voice low and firm.

'And me?' Anthony asked. 'Us?'

Becca smiled. 'I don't know what to say.'

'Say yes, Becca Valentine.'

'Yes,' she said.

'Yes,' Samuel repeated, his expression serious.

* * *

'How long until Lucy's date?' I asked Thomas.

'A couple of weeks,' he said.

'Perfect.'

'I wish we were with her.'

'Me too, but at least we're together.'

He looked at me, and there were tears in his eyes. If we'd had hands, we would have held them.

AUTHOR LETTER

Dear Reader,

The book you've just read (or are just about to read, perhaps) started life as a dream. It was hazy, and the only thing I remembered from it was that there were these people, these figures, who were waiting to be conceived. It was about a life before this life. The Beforelife. For years, I mulled it over while writing other things. And then eventually a plot began to form. A group of potential siblings, a love triangle, a battle for existence.

When you have children, it's hard to imagine having any children other than the ones you had. Even someone like me, who doesn't believe in an afterlife or a beforelife, can almost imagine they had always been around. That they were meant to be. It's also interesting to think about the children you might have had, and didn't. About how different the family dynamic would have been if you'd had more children, or fewer. Or different children.

I had breast cancer when I was pregnant with my second child, and found out that I have a gene mutation that puts me at high risk of both breast and ovarian cancer. I asked to have my ovaries removed, to lessen the risk, but my doctors were cautious. I had two children and I'd never wanted more. My husband felt the same way. But they kept suggesting I might change my mind. I never have, and the operation went ahead, but occasionally I wonder about it. Have I never changed my mind because I know I can't? I don't think so, but there's no way of knowing for sure.

I hope you enjoy getting to know Eliza Valentine and her siblings. And Becca, of course. Families are complicated things, and theirs is no different. I always feel so lucky when readers take these people I've created into their hearts.

With love, Laura

ACKNOWLEDGEMENTS

This book is very special to me. I say that about every book, and it's always true, but this one is a bit of a departure from what I've written before, and that kind of thing takes a leap of faith (and a supportive agent and publishing team). *The Beforelife of Eliza Valentine* began life as a dream, many years ago, in which I had this sense of people waiting around, watching their mothers, before being conceived. I knew instantly that I wanted to use it in a novel, but it took me years to settle on how. When I did, I wrote it, and rewrote it, and rewrote it, but it didn't get as far as publication. Thank you to Kate Evans, my previous agent, who championed it tirelessly at that time.

When I came to sign my second contract with my fabulous publishers, Boldwood, my agent showed my editor this book. Thank you to Jo Williamson for believing in my strange little homeless novel, and thank you to Isobel Akenhead for being open to the idea of a book about a life before this life, despite it marking a slightly different direction for me. Enormous thanks to everyone at Boldwood who work so efficiently and effectively. You're the best.

Thank you to my writing friends, who never make it feel like a competition. Lauren North, Nikki Smith and Zoe Lea, in particular, because they see me through every idea, every draft, every success, and every failure. This book is for them. Thank you to my non-writing friends for listening and supporting and making me laugh every day. Thank you to the admins and members of The Bookload for all the bookish joy.

Thank you to my family. My parents, Sue and Phil Pearson, and my sister, Rachel Timmins. My in-laws, Sue and George Herbert. Paul, for believing in me so consistently. Joseph and Elodie, for teaching me just how much I didn't know before about love. And Phoebe, for her company (if you could sit anywhere other than the keyboard, that would be great).

ABOUT THE AUTHOR

Laura Pearson is the author of the #1 bestseller *The Last List of Mabel Beaumont*. She founded The Bookload on Facebook and has had several pieces published in the Guardian and the Telegraph.

Sign up to Laura Pearson's newsletter to read the first chapter of her upcoming novel and a free short story.

Visit Laura's website: www.laurapearsonauthor.com

Follow Laura on social media here:

facebook.com/laurapearson22

x.com/laurapauthor

instagram.com/laurapauthor

bookbub.com/authors/laura-pearson

ALSO BY LAURA PEARSON

The Last List of Mabel Beaumont

I Wanted You To Know

Missing Pieces

The Day Shelley Woodhouse Woke Up

Nobody's Wife

The Beforelife of Eliza Valentine

Boldwood

Boldwood Books is an award-winning fiction publishing company seeking out the best stories from around the world.

Find out more at www.boldwoodbooks.com

Join our reader community for brilliant books, competitions and offers!

Follow us
@BoldwoodBooks
@TheBoldBookClub

Sign up to our weekly
deals newsletter

https://bit.ly/BoldwoodBNewsletter

Printed in Great Britain
by Amazon

48207056R00165